CRYSTALS FOR BEGINNERS

Discover the Healing Powers of Crystals and Healing Stones

Crystal Lee

"Copyright 2018 by Crystal Lee-All rights reserved. No part of this book may be reproduced or transmitted in any form or by any means, electronic or mechanical, including photocopying, recording or by any information storage and retrieval system without written permission of the publisher, except for the inclusion of brief quotations in a review.

TABLE OF CONTENTS

Introduction 1

Chapter 1 *The History Of Healing Stones* 2

Chapter 2 *Chakras* 18

Chapter 3 *Negative Energy Cleansing* 26

Chapter 4 *Incorporating Crystals And Their Knowledge Into Your Daily Life* 34

Chapter 5 *Starting A Crystal Collection* 49

Chapter 6 *Different Types Of Energy Healing* 57

Chapter 7 *Types Of Healing Crystals* 61

Chapter 8 *Crystal Mining And Collecting For Yourself* 132

Chapter 9 *Benefits Of Crystal And Energy Healing* 135

Conclusion 139

Description 140

INTRODUCTION

Congratulations on downloading *Crystals for Beginners* and thank you for doing so. This is a beginner's book for those wanting to begin or expand their knowledge of crystals and their unique healing properties. There are a lot of ways to improve your health and peace of mind these days, crystal healing is an extremely relaxing and educational way to do so.

There is a deep profound link between body, mind, and spirit. Disruptions affect all aspects of life, including relationships, career, hobbies, emotions, and even physical health. Sometimes we overreact or have no idea how to explain the way we're feeling. Crystal healing covers the concept that you can find balance to your emotional state with therapies that exists beyond pharmaceuticals. These therapies can provide maximum benefit for you and your mind and can be a lot less expensive than other treatments.

The following chapters of this book will cover basic approaches and ideal ways to bring positive energy into your life using crystals, energy healing, self-awareness, and the knowledge that connects these to our essential being. They will also discuss healthy ways of releasing energy, chakra balancing, the importance of understanding/practicing crystals medicine, and everything you need to know about the benefits stones provide for the human condition. There is a lot to learn about crystals and how they can interact with your body.

There are plenty of books on this subject on the market, thanks again for choosing *Crystals for beginners*. I hope that the information provided in this book will help you develop how to ignite your spirituality and improve your quality of life, as well as help you get a better understanding of your spiritual being and how crystals can bring many benefits to your life, please enjoy!

CHAPTER 1
The History Of Healing Stones

What are crystals? Crystals are natural elements that originally come from the earth. They are formed through a solidification process of chemicals and have an internal arrangement of atoms and molecules that are regularly repeating. A true crystal has an organized formation of unit cells that form a unique lattice pattern called a crystal system. These lattices appear within healing stones.

Healing stones are proven to of been around since the late 19th and early 20th centuries. Throughout history, ancient cultures around the world have too aligned, clear and reinvented their energy, spirit, and overall health using healing crystals and stones. Stones of all type have become again more popular since the '80s; there has lately been a rise in interest in the healing properties and powers that exist beyond medical drugs. They are mainly used for a source of spiritual healing and as a conduit of personal cleansing. Healing stones are one of the most common yet not often discussed holistic therapies that exist. The Philosophy on modern Crystal healing is based on traditional concepts adopted from Asian cultures, the most notable-the Chinese concept of life-energy (chi or qi).

Ancient

Crystals are millions of years old pieces of rock formed in the earliest part of the formation of the earth. The oldest crystal ever discovered is called Zircon and dates back to 4.4 billion years.

Ancient Samaria

Historical reference shows that around the 4th millennium B.C. crystals were used. The Sumerians believed that every crystal was linked to the energy of the planets and therefore used the crystals in magic formulas. They would also use certain stones for cosmetic purposes, such as eyeshadow, lipstick, and contour, just as we do now. All of which was documented in an ancient text.

30,000 Years Ago

Some of the oldest amulets in Britain made from Baltic Amber date back to about 30 000 years ago. A gem belonged to Timur Lenk in the 1300s and was named after he died. He is best known as the Islamic conqueror of Eastern and Central Asia. Timur Ruby's 361 carat is an impressive red gem. The distance to Britain that the crystal traveled shows its importance and value to the people of that time.
Names and dates carved on the stone show that it belonged to five Indian rulers later on. One of them was Shah Jehan, the Taj Mahal builder. In Britain, amulets were primarily used to show wealth, power, and high status. The Timur Ruby was one of the treasures brought to England from India in 1850.

Paleolithic Era

In the grave sights around Belgium and Switzerland, jet beads, bracelets, and necklaces were discovered. Other crystals and stones had mainly been used in the manufacturing of everyday functional tools. Such as fire flint, hunting arrowheads, housing parts, axes, wheels, and spears.

Ancient India

In ancient Ayurvedic documents such as the Hindu Vedas, the use of healing crystals was well documented. The people of India especially loved diamonds, which they believed to have great strength and endurance to withstand adversity. They liked Sapphire for clarity and balance of mind, as well as Jasper for harmony and the sex life.

Ancient Egypt

Egyptians have been referred to in history as one of the first people to decorate themselves with crystals to prevent disease and negative energy. The crystals would be used for decoration, religious purposes, good luck charms and more. It was strongly believed that the Egyptians were very spiritually enveloped in the stones, they connected certain stones with specific gods and used the crystals in burials, which they thought would help the deceased to find their way into the afterlife.

Ancient Greece

Most names we give to crystals are originally from the Greek language. Surprising enough, the Greek word " Krystillos," which translates to Ice, comes from the word crystal. Greek culture worshipped Athena, the god of war. Before a battle, soldiers crushed hematite up and rubbed it on themselves believing it to make them "invincible."

Jewelry was also very popular in ancient Greece, the earliest necklaces come from 1,500 BC incorporating mainly Emeralds, Rubies, Sapphires, Pearls, and Carnelians. The Greeks believed that amethyst had many powers, including protection against intoxication. The word " amethyst" is derived from the Greek word " amethyst."

Native Americans

In both North and South America, Native Americans believed heavily in the healing powers of crystals. For them, Turquoise was the most sacred of all crystals, used primarily for personal protection, but also for spiritual and emotional healing. Of course, the diverse northern and southern cultures have practiced numerous unique crystal healing techniques.

North America – For Mayans, one of the most famous civilizations in ancient North

America – the fire opal and Jade were considered to be very valuable and important in Mayan culture. It is also related to breath. The Aztec civilization also used healing crystals. These civilizations were one of North America 's first ancient cultures to use crystals to cure physical diseases and emotional imbalances.

South America – Although there is little information about the use of Norte Chico crystals, there are countless references to the use of crystals as jewelry by Norte Chico's leaders. The Inca civilization used a wide variety of crystals to heal. Incas used large amounts of quartz and jade for healing.

Ancient China

Jade was the favored healing stone of ancient Chinese people and has been mined in China since the Stone Age. In fact, most of the major gemstones/healing crystals were originally mined in China.

Renaissance

Mystical healers started to learn how to draw and use the energy of crystals for a variety of health conditions. Literature has described how healing crystals were used in medicine and some famous authors, including Binghen, Saxo, and Mandeville, often mentioned that the benefits of crystals became much more powerful when used in conjunction with herbal healing practices. During this period, crystals were regarded as endowed with 'virtues' that could easily be destroyed. Some mystics believed that even if there was original sin, some gemstones could lose their virtue. Others believed that a virtue inherent in crystals could be lost if it was misused or if it was handled by someone with bad intentions.

In this light, crystals were used with utmost caution and care in the Renaissance. Before their powers were harnessed, stones were cleaned, consecrated, and sanctified– a practice reflected in the cleaning and programming process of crystals before use.

Some crystals in the period of renaissance were particularly valuable. A gem in the possession of Henry III was allegedly stolen by his chief justiciar. The gem was said to have been given to the King of Wales – Henry's enemy. This angered Henry, and the justiciar was branded a criminal since the gem he has stolen was considered most powerful, capable of making its wearer invincible.

Mythology

Amazing enough crystals and gems, rare and beautiful played an important role in ancient mythology. People used them in the hope of transmitting some of the properties of the crystals they used: strength, beauty, magic power, etc.

Crystals in Technology Past

Military radios – in World War II, the military used quartz oscillators to control the frequency of two-way radio transmissions, the oscillators were highly precise but difficult to mass-produce.

Consumer electronics – electronic manufacturers use electronic-grade manufactured quartz in computer circuits, cell phones, and similar equipment. CNet even reports that quartz in its natural form and other piezoelectric crystals were used in their raw form to manufacture an experimental rudimentary computer that transmitted or received signals such as randomized sound or light

Watches – due to the precision of quartz oscillators, they are used in watches, which require precision in timekeeping. Only a tiny piece of quartz is used, according to the watch company, but it oscillates so precisely that it can be accurate to a few seconds per year.

Holy Texts and the Energy Connection

Holy, religious books from various cultures discuss the importance of life force (energy) in the spiritual, emotional, and physical health of humankind.

In the Bible, it says, "that energy is God's energy, any energy deep within you, God himself willing and working at what will give him the most pleasure. (Philippians 2:13) In the Gospel of John, Jesus heals the sick using the energy of God and prayer."

The Hindu Vidas speak of prana, the life force that flows through all living things. According to the Yajur Veda, "there are 11 in the vital energy (prana) existing by their own virtue (ear, skin, eye, tongue, nose, speech, hands, legs, two organs of excretion, and mind.)" These are body parts of volition and perception, not reality.

Buddha also noted energy in defining Seven Factors of enlightenment: mindfulness, investigation of the dharma (cosmic laws), energy, joy, relaxation, and tranquility, concentration and equanimity.

Those who follow Kabbalah, the mystical branch of Judaism, study the Zohar, a collection of comments that reveal the Torah's spiritual essence. The Zohar notes that when the Tora portion is known as "Pinchas" is read aloud once each year during the Sabbath, those who listen with an open heart and remorse for prior misdeeds (even without any knowledge of Hebrew) may experience a great, healing light.

Crystals in Technology Today

One of the most intriguing and extraordinary features of certain crystals is that they produce a permeable electric charge. This is known as the piezoelectric effect and was discovered by Pierre and Jacques Curie in the early 19th century. Eventually, with the development of technology and science, it was possible to put this discovery to use.

Crystals transmit a piezoelectric charge that impacts the biomagnetic fields of the body. Crystals reflect and withdraw light rays like infrared and ultraviolet rays, which are both used to repair and sanitize the body. Crystals also have the power to carry information. Even from a scientific perspective, it seems possible natural crystals can influence physical functioning.

Pyroelectric effect: pyroelectric crystals such as tourmaline generate electrical current when heated or cooled, according to scientists, many applications exist for pyroelectricity, for example, power conversion and infrared detection, among others.

Piezoelectric effect: the piezoelectric effect occurs when no conducting crystals generate an electrical charge when put under mechanical stress. Quartz is one crystal that demonstrates piezoelectricity, which makes it popular for use in devices like radios, watches, and other digital integrated circuits.

It would be very hard to imagine life without crystals since they play a vital role in electronics and optical industries. It is safe to say technological development without crystals would not be possible.

Examples of Modern Science with Crystals

Solar cells – powering instruments from calculators to place vehicles.

Transistors – based on the same types of materials and crystals as solar cells. Transistors can negate electron flow, and amplify radio signals, as well as act as a digital switch.

Liquid Crystals – wrist watches, some types of clocks and pocket calculators.

Protein Structures – crystals help solve different protein structures, which is extremely useful in biochemistry.

Pencils – graphite is a type of crystal.

Computer Chips – silicones form the basis for all microelectronics, such as computer chips.

Optical Equipment – some optical equipment is made from crystals.

CD's and DVD's – crystalline solids in them enable us to write and store information on them.

Myths about Crystals

Myth #1: It's all in my head.
The crystals work is designed to take you out of your head and make you feel like it. Crystals do not require rationalization or explanation; they give you the opportunity to experience them. If you're worried its all in your head, stop thinking and experience the sensations the crystals provide. You can rationalize it later.

Myth #2: If crystals can help, they can hard.
Crystals vibrate with energy that can entrain to your energy. Intention and mindset play big roles in this. If you expect crystals to harm you, that may wind up being your exact experience, this- this is true of anything. Your beliefs always play an important role in your results and experience, whether you use crystals or placebo or medication. In general, if you approach the crystals with the intention of shifting vibration for your highest and greatest good, it is highly unlikely you will be hurt in any way.

Myth #3: I have to be spiritual or new age to use crystals.
To use crystals, you don't have to be New Age, spiritual or religious, nor do they run counter to any religion or spirituality, all you need is an open mind and a sincere desire for change that serves your highest and greatest good.

Myth #4: I don't need to cleanse my crystals.
Since crystals tend to absorb energy, it is important to clean them so that unwanted energy is removed. If you use them consistently, energy can build up and you will have to clean up more frequently if the energy is negative.

Myth #5: expensive crystals are more powerful.
Quartz is one of the most common and inexpensive crystals, it's also one of the most powerful. The amount of money you spend on crystals really doesn't have anything to do with how effective it is. What matters is how a crystal affects your energy, and some of the least expensive crystals may be exactly what you need.

Crystal Remedies for Certain Emotions

When you are dealing with mental, emotional, or spiritual issues, you may find remedies in this chapter quite helpful.

Abandonment – There may be feelings of abandonment resulting from a recent breakup, loss of family members or somebody important to you. You can feel lost, alone, empty. Use this mantra to remember that you are the real source of unconditional love.

"I give myself unconditional love and receive unconditional love from the universe."

Meditation – Meditate using this manta and while holding a rose quartz crystal, the stone of unconditional love. Picture yourself in a very happy, loving state of mind. Continue until you feel peace.

Stones that help feeling abandonment:

- Amazonite for healing emotional pain.
- Garnet for healing issues of belonging.
- Carnelian for self-empowerment.

Abuse – Whether emotional, physical, or mental, this can leave lasting scars. Many people carry the effects of abuse with them, essentially sometimes becoming their own tormentor long after the abuse has ceased. If you are experiencing current abuse, seeking professional help is an important first step.

"I release the pain of my past for a more positive and loving future."

Meditation – Close your eyes and allow yourself to feel the grief and pain. Take note of where you feel the pain, then use breathing exercises to release the pain. Exhale and repeat the mantra until you feel peace.

Stones that help with abuse:

- Garnet for a sense of belonging and identity.
- Carnelian for personal power.

- Yellow tigers eye for self-esteem.
- Rose Quartz for unconditional love.

Addiction – Whether you are addicted to an activity, an idea, a person, or even a substance, addiction can quickly throw you and your life completely out of balance. Supporting yourself spiritually and emotionally can help ease that process.

"I am free of my desire for _____. I release it, and it releases me."

Meditation – Addiction can make you very off balanced, so meditating on the mantra while lying with stones can be helpful to restore your balance. Focus on your sacral and throat chakra for they deal with willpower.

Stones that help with addiction:

- Labradorite for detoxification.
- Amethyst for its sober properties.

Anger – A natural and acceptable emotion that everybody has. When we allow ourselves to fully experience anger, it can easily pass through our body's and dissipate. However, sometimes we get stuck in anger until it hardens into resentment. Know that holding onto anger only harms you.

"I breathe in peace. I release anger."

Meditation – Place both hands over your solar plexus chakra, repeat your mantra, and picture energy flowing out of your body through your nose.

Stones that help with anger:

- Carnelian for a calm and grounded feeling.
- Amber to absorb negativity.
- Black tourmaline for positive energy flow.

Anxiety – While it is natural to feel anxious from time to time, persistent anxiety can keep you from living your best life. Anxiety can take many forms such as Phobias and social anxiety. Anxiety resides in the Root Chakra.

"I relax into infinite serenity."

Meditation – Sit quietly while holding a stone that relates to the Root Chakra. Visualize peace flowing inside of you and say the mantra.

Stones that help with anxiety:

- Blue lace agate for reflective calming properties.
- Lapis lazuli for grounding and relief.
- Black Tourmaline for absorbing negative energy.

Accepting Change – Most people find change difficult because of the fear of the unknown and getting too comfortable. Change is a necessary and natural part of life; you cannot grow without it.

"I am grateful for the change in my life because it serves as a source of positive empowerment."

Meditation – Breathe deeply while visualizing pure white energy flowing throughout you, repeat mantra at the same time.

Stones that help accepting change:

- Watermelon Tourmaline for clarity to your situation.
- Prehnite to amplify inner strength and accepting new circumstances.

Compassion – Intricately linked to unconditional love, which is connected to the Heart Chakra. It enables you to feel deeply for another and act toward them with kindness and care.

"The spark of divinity in me recognizes the spark of divinity in you."

Meditation – Sit or lie with your eyes closed and visualize the person for whom you want to cultivate compassion for. Repeat mantra while visualizing pure energy coming from your heart.

Stones that help with compassion:

- Rose Quarts for loving energy.
- Celestite for healing relationships.

Confidence – Comes from the Solar Plexus chakra, where you foster your sense of personal identity and self-esteem to grow more confident, pay close attention to these two chakras, learning who you are and then living that truth with integrity.

"I exude confidence because I know I am living my truth."

Meditation – Visualize yourself going about your day with the confidence that you are living within your integrity. Repeat mantra and try to be detailed in the visualization.

Stones that help with confidence:

- Moonstone for boosting confidence.
- Hematite for building confidence.

Depression – Depression can affect your mind, body, spirit, and cause lingering physical pain and ennui that keeps us from living a vibrant, joyful, and productive life.

"I seek out and enjoy all the pleasure and happiness available to me in my daily life."

Meditation – Speak your mantra loud and add, "I am grateful for" to the end and state, what you are grateful for.

Stones that help with depression

- Amber for spiritual healing.
- Smoky Quartz for absorbing bad energy.

Eating Disorders – They appear to be about food but they tend to have emotional, spiritual, and physical roots. It is important you seek professional help as well if you have an eating disorder.

"my body, mind, and spirit are beautiful, and I bless myself with unconditional love."

Meditation – Any time you feel compulsive eating disorder behaviors stop for a moment, close your eyes, and take big, deep, and long breath. Repeat mantra.
Stones for eating disorders:
Rose Quartz for unconditional self-love
Carnelian for self-acceptance and motivation

Emotional Balance – maintain emotion balance can help you stay steady throughout the day which allows you to think clearly, access your creativity, experience gratitude, and enjoy your life.

"I allow my emotions to serve as opportunities for growth, and then I return to my center."

Meditation – Daily mindfulness meditation can help your overall balance of emotions, when thoughts come up, simply allow them to pass by quickly.

Stones that help with emotional balance:

- Garnet for emotional foundation
- Malachite for rebalancing

Rainbow Fluorite for balancing all of the chakras

Achieving Goals – Setting and achieving goals is an important part of your life path. While walking a straight line to a goal may seem ideal, sometimes the detours on the way to our goals offer the most valuable lessons and insights.

"Anything blocking my path to my goals dissolves at this moment."

Meditation – Speak the mantra and visualize yourself living your life when you have achieved your goals. What will life look like? Visualize and repeat.

Stones that help to achieve goals:

- Carnelian for goal-oriented action
- Clear Quartz for manifestation.

Grounding – Grounding keeps us connected to the earth, which is our source of support and strength. You should ground yourself whenever you feel out of sorts, it can keep you focused and centered.

"I honor the jewel with the lotus bloom."

Meditation – Sit comfortably whole holding grounding stones and repeat the mantra.

Stones that help grounding:

- Lodestone for grounding visualization
- Black Tourmaline for connection to the earth
- Obsidian for self-love and reflection

Indecisiveness – Life would be so much easier if you could make instant decisions every moment of the day, but some decisions are more difficult to make.
"I am in tune with what I need, and trust my intuition to guide me to the right choices."

Meditation-Focus your attention to your third eye chakra, and consider the decisions you need to make and repeat the mantra.

Stones that help with indecisiveness:

- Amethyst for paying attention
- Ametrine for intuitive problem solving

Insomnia – Many things can come from this sleep disorder insomnia such as stress, physical pain, inconsistent sleep patterns, and environmental issues.

"I release the stress of my day and drift off into a deep, refreshing sleep."

Meditation – At bedtime, use progressive relaxation and mindfulness to clear your mind of stressful thoughts and promote relaxation and restfulness in your body. Use visual meditation to help you drift off.

<u>**Stones that help insomnia:**</u>

- Amethyst for relaxation and tranquility
- Moonstone for sleep aid

Laziness – Sometimes we form a lack of initiative, as a reaction of doing things we have to do but don't want to do.

"I am energized to take action to make things happen in my life."

Meditation – Repeat this mantra to yourself, visualize yourself taking action on things you have resisted, allowing the visualization to carry through to the results of having taken action.

<u>**Stones that help with laziness:**</u>

- Calcite for overcoming inactions
- Rainbow fluorite for focusing your energy

Obsession – Obsessive thought arrives from anxiety while compulsion is a repetitive behavior that helps relieve some anxiety.

"I embrace the uncertainty of life, and choose to live peacefully within it."

Meditation – A problem that arises from obsession, compulsion is when your brain gets stuck in a thought loop.

Stones that help with obsession:

- Ametrine for controlling thoughts and emotions
- Herkimer diamond to relieve stress
- Citrine for visualizing energy
- Amethyst for tranquility and peace of mind.

CHAPTER 2
Chakras

Chakras are seven energy sites in the body which help to regulate all of its systems, from immune function to the organ system and emotions. They are directly associated with the nine endocrine glands. Each chakra is specifically placed throughout your body, and every chakra has its own frequency of vibration, color, and governs processes that make you human. Crystals are directly associated with our Chakras and can be extremely beneficial to our health when used correctly.

Chakras have the ability to close, therefore allowing the inward and outward flow of energy. There are two major energy flows that contribute to your chakras ' balance. An upward flow from the magnetic field of the earth and a downward flow from a universal energy that incorporates all. It is said that these two currents balance the entire system.

Before you dive deep into the meaning of chakras you must understand one thing: You are energy. All living things are created by and compromised by energy. Optimally, the function of your energy centers keeps you psychologically, emotionally, physically and spiritually balanced inside.

Chakra Imbalance

How do you identify a Chakra blockage?
Understanding what your chakras are and what they're for should help make it easier for you to determine whether they're under attack.
There are specific ways to identify each chakra:

Blockages to the Root Chakra: When you are feeling stuck in a situation, a sense of sluggishness, persistent problems that plague different areas of your life (financial, job, long-term, relationships), a feeling of abandonment by family and friends; a feeling of just barely getting by in life with a foreseeable end, or a feeling of lack of control over your body, your fitness, and your health.

Blockages to the Sacral Chakra: When you are having difficulties expressing yourself sexually, fear of exploring your sexual facet, challenges tapping into your sensual side, moving from relationship to relationship, struggling to feel comfortable in your own body, and the inability to believe that others might feel attracted to you as you are.

Blockages to the Solar Plexus Chakra: When you have a feeling of powerlessness over your situation, giving others power over yourself in order to maintain peace in your relationships, difficulty acting on your aspirations and goals since you feel too weak to act on them, and difficulty expressing yourself in front of a crowd or audience.

Blockages to the Heart Chakra: When you are constantly pleasing others in order to attain a feeling of being loved, excessively guarding your heart to the point of refusing to let other people in, holding on to your feelings of anger and disappointment when others around you fail to meet your expectations of them, and challenges in giving too much compassion or too little.

Blockages to the Throat Chakra: When you have developed a fear of telling others what you think or feel, allowing other people and conforming to the majority in order to avoid bringing your uniqueness to light, and feelings of frustration because no one seems to understand how you feel or what you think.

Blockages to the Third Eye Chakra: When you have feelings of disconnectedness with your intuition or weakness, difficulty or inability of making decisions for yourself without sound evidence and information to guide you to the right choice, feelings of frustration at frequently making mistakes with decisions that involve the future.

Blockages to the Crown Chakra: When you have feelings of loneliness, insignificance, and meaninglessness, a strong attachment or affinity with material possessions, a lack of guidance from any higher being, and a general feeling of not being able to maximize the capabilities of your cognition.

A Chakra Imbalance Can Affect

How much power flows through the systems of the chakras.
When energy is blocked or closed, chakras are ineffective.
Chakras are overactive if the flow of energy is increased excessively and not properly regulated.

Chakra Balancing

The process to restore the harmonious energy flow through the chakra system. Whenever a chakra is blocked, underactive, or overactive, it can make you off balance. You see, your body wants a strong balance in your chakras. They may actually have negative effects on the person if they are underactive or overactive and may be counterproductive to the energy body and chakra healing process.

What to Expect When the Chakras Are Functioning Properly

Balance, Equilibrium.
Distinction between the different energy and frequency quality of each chakra.
Appropriate polarity and direction.

Chakra Cleansing

The whole blockage and/or negativity must be removed in order to restore the positive balance to the energy center involved. Energy healing is the most common method for balancing chakras, which can include:
Tai Chi
Conscious breathing exercises
Reiki
Chakra meditation

Yoga
Aromatherapy
Music
Positive affirmations

The Seven Chakras

Crown Chakra (Brahmarandra) – Pink for spirituality. Located at the top of your head.
<u>Representation</u>: Associated with issues involving poor, shallow relationships, difficulties exploring new experiences and places, repressed emotions, weak connection with spirituality, and the ego.

Third eye Chakra (Sahasrara) – Dark blue for awareness. Located between your eyebrows.
<u>Representation</u>: Associated with issues involving sleep, mood, feelings of paranoia, depression, and anxiety. And relates to your intuition, imagination, and cognitive abilities.

Throat Chakra (Vishuddhi) – Light blue for communication. Right in-between your collar bones.
<u>Representation</u>: Associated with issues involving the inability to express feelings and personal truth to oneself, and dealing with other people's deception.

Heart Chakra (Anahata) – Green for love and healing. Located right over your heart.
<u>Representation</u>: Associated with issues involving relationships, emotions, peace, and threats to our emotions.

Solar Plexus Chakra (Manipuraka) – Yellow for wisdom and power.
Located from the center of your belly button to the center of your chest.
<u>Representation</u>: Associated with issues involving personal preconceptions, public relations, and self-value. As well as self-confidence, self-esteem, and self-worth.

Sacral Chakra (Swadhisthana) – Orange for sexuality and creativity.
Located right below the belly button.
<u>Representation</u>: Associated with issues involving the pleasure response, the feeling of abundance and well-being. As well as creativity and your ability to adapt.

Root Chakra (Muladhara) – Red for basic and trust.
Located at the very base of your spine.
<u>Representation</u>: Associated with issues involving survival such as the basic biological needs and financial concerns. As well as proving you with a foundation that should make you feel grounded.

Healing the Aura

The Aura is a multi-layered energy field covering the human body. It appears to form a shape around the physical body and project colors. Some people are said to be able to see the Aura, others cannot. Auras are believed to be caused by the vibrations that surround every material object. Light energy is drawn into this kind of egg that acts as a prism and transforms light into its elements of color.

Aura Layers – They are seven major aura layers with an interconnected relationship between the aura layers and the body's seven main chakras:

The Etheric layer – It is an indicator of a strong weakened physical health; it is primarily linked to the root/base chakra and is the auric layer that is most easily seen. It can also be seen around plants, trees, and animals. Good health is depicted by a uniform bright band of light surrounding and contouring the human body. Poor health is indicated by a bulge in the physical layer near the affected area. It looks a bit like lumps and bumps. Most hereditary disorders and old injuries can also be located in the physical layer

The Emotional body – This layer is beyond the etheric field and ranges from 1 to 3 inches. It acts as a storage of thoughts and feelings and our personal relationships. It is linked strongly to the sacral chakra and contains bright energy blobs and healthy colors.

These primary colors are emitted in the same way that the emotions change in a' mood' ring.

The Mental body – This layer is beyond the emotional body and extends away from the body. It shows a person's thoughts and attitudes and refers to mental activity. Not only does it radiate energy from the environment. This body connects to the plexus chakra of energy.

The Astral body – Lies beyond the mind. It is associated with our relationships with people around us and closely linked to the chakra of the heart. It's the connection between the spiritual world and the physical world. Information about past and present life is contained in this layer because it stores good and bad experiences and life lessons.

The Casual Body – Lies beyond the astral field. It displays a person's ability on the conscious or intellectual level. It is associated with the power of the self-expression and connected to the throat chakra.

The Celestial Body – It is linked to universal wisdom and the sense of awareness of the self of life. Also connected to the Third-eye chakra. It is the layer through which you can experience spiritual ecstasy and the ways of religious ceremony.

The Ketheric Body – Vibrates at the highest frequency and is most difficult to fully understand. This is where we experience divine wisdom and our oneness with the universe around us.

Aura Colors

The most common colors seen around people and their different meanings are listed below, depending on your health, mood and spiritual connection.

Maroon: daily vocation, ambition, life work.

Dark red: hate, anger, passion, violence.

Bright Red: life, passion, vitality, energy.

Orange: artistry, vitality, creativity, ambition.

Orange-red: energy, sexuality.

Yellow: happiness, optimism, purity.

Pink: pregnancy, unconditional love, love, femininity.

Green: intellect, jealousy, nature connection.

Dirty Green: illness, spite, envy, jealousy.

Blue: higher connection, spiritual feelings, teacher.

Purple: deep spiritual interests, ideals.

Grey: tiredness, illness, lack of spiritual connection.

Brown: Usually indicate lethargy and an indication of physical problems about to manifest.

Black: Extreme illness, addictions, close to death. It is often seen on those who are either victims of abuse or who are substance abusers.

Silver: angels, unconditional love, strong connection to a higher power, master qualities.

Gold: purity, connection to a higher power.

Energy Impurities in the Aura

Aura impurities are energy areas in the aura that are not required for the regular, healthy energy functioning of the field. They can be described as areas of unwanted stagnant energy build up in the aura, energies that block or inhibit the free tide of energy in the field of energy.

They are often found in and directly above the body's surface, in contact with the body, usually around the head, face, neck, shoulder, chest, and abdomen. The removal of these unhealthy energy sources also helps to treat and prevent physical illness.

Cleaning the Aura

The aura energy can be felt most easily in your hands and fingers. To feel the aura, run your hands vigorously for about one minute and hold your hands a little apart, palms facing each other. You will feel a heat pass between your hands. Take one hand and run it, palm down, along with the front of your body, without actually touching your body. You will feel a similar heat. This energy can be used for the physical body's protection. Surround yourself with a white light shower with a strong, golden shell.

CHAPTER 3
Negative Energy Cleansing

Why cleanse your house and body? There are basic principles governing how energy flows, we are all made up of energy and you as a human being are perfectly able to understand and work with it. Every day you come across opportunities to absorb bad energy. The more familiar you become with your NEA the more familiar you will become with conscious ways to release the energy. Negative Energy Absorption (NEA) is an actually serious condition that occurs with every human being on a daily basis. It is when a person absorbs either subconsciously or consciously, unhealthy and negative energy. It is heavily related to our own vibrational frequencies; you can catch a bad vibe very easily. While you intake negativity energy, you also intake positive and healthy energy. So the outcomes aren't all bad, there often is a balance. But when there isn't? What do you do?

How to detect negative energy. Without attention and constant care, things naturally move from order to disorder unless we put things way were they belong. You definitely don't have to be a master healer to notice if the energy around you is a little bit off. Simply take a second to really take in the vibe around you and decide how to go about your cleanse.

Removing negative energy from your body and home. Sometimes we say that we have to talk a break or go for a walk to clear our heads. If you've ever felt that way, you have recognized that your mental energy body was blocked and needed to be cleansed. Clearing your energy body is just like that. You consciously examine what is residing within you. Then you can decide what you want to keep and cultivate and what you want to release based on your free will. Our energy bodies could look like a hoarder's house, so full that it is hard to move around and be organized. This is why clearing takes a little more effort and time when you first begin to work.

How often should you cleanse? Negative energy cleansing is not something we do just once, it is an ongoing activity. A lot of people in this age are not educated in good energy maintenance, as we walk through our days we are bombarded with other people's energy in the form of thoughts or emotions.

In What Ways Can You Cleanse?

Sage has been considered a sacred plant for thousands of years. This multipurpose plant was used for cleansing, healing, ritual ceremonies, and even smoked. Today practitioners continue to use sage to help restore one's basic health. It is said to neutralize your energy field. Adding Frankincense, Palo Santo wood, or Copal incense works wonderfully to balance out the intensity of the sage. Aromatherapy has holistic benefits that can help heal or lift your spirits. Practicing Yoga helps you exercise your soul with mantras, movements, and breathing exercises. Establish meditation practice, it helps reset, rest, and recharge your mind, soul, and body. Prioritize self-help such as eating habits, exercise, healthy sleeping patterns, and doing things you genuinely enjoy. Explore holistic health because you can always dig deeper into remedies that just might speak to your soul or be exactly what you need. And last but not least believe in the unexplainable because sometimes trying to analyze things that don't have a direct answer can be unhealthy and especially tiring.

Movement-Based Techniques

Movement is a great and easy way to move energy around or get rid of lingering negative energy. Movement can be subtle and vigorous.

Mountain Pose – Yoga's mountain pose might seem like more of a non-movement activity. However, the act of assuming and holding the pose includes subtle but important movement. You stand with your intention. Make sure to keep your back straight, air flowing, and muscles tightened.

Walking – When done with intention, walking is a wonderful practice. With each step of your walk, you should feel the energy that you are focusing on the break-up and begin to move down to your feet. Walk until you feel clearer than before. While walking, try to maintain a strong, aligned posture because it is really good for removing intense and negative energy when done right. Pay attention to what your body is doing while you're walking. Our bodies are a great source of wisdom and can tell us a lot about our energy body. Bring attention to the areas and see if there is energy that needs work or cleansing.

Dancing – Dancing is a natural energy mover. There are various kinds of dancing, as well as reasons and venues where people go just to dance. Even going to a concert or party and getting your blood pumping can be apart of spiritual energy cleansing practice. Any kind of dancing can be apart of energy maintenance.

Setting your intention before dancing is something a lot of people like to do. Dancing is primal for us and we have to learn to trust our body. Sometimes these less consciously controlled methods are great choices, especially when you aren't really sure what is wrong or where it is wrong.

Yin Yoga – Westerners often engage in activities like tai chi and yoga for physical benefits. However, these practices are deeply rooted in energy work. In their entirety, they are clear, contain, and activate. When practiced mindfully, they are awesome for aura cleansing and energy health. Yin Yoga focuses on holding passive poses for long periods, generally from one to five for beginners. These long poses can physically tend beyond our larger, more visible anatomy and treat to the deeper anatomy. Yin Yoga is helpful for releasing because so many of the poses create free space for energy to flow in the body. The principle of this technique is, "as above, so below".

When we move our physical bodies, we move our energy. Stagnation is extremely prolonged and inappropriate stillness. Anxiety is intensely vibrating energy; your body can help maintain the appropriate vibration for you in almost any circumstance. Keep stagnant energy and anxiety out of your life and make sure to keep your energy clear and flowing by moving your body properly.

Sound – using sound is an easy way to move your energy around by raising vibration, creating space, and breaking up stagnant energy. While this technique is mostly used for physical spaces or while doing energy work for others, you can also use it on yourself. Remember, intention always matters. Traditional methods of using sounds to get rid of negative energy include rattles, drums, gongs, bells, singing bowls, and clapping. You can also use singing and chanting, but those are often found more of use for energy cultivation. Common sound techniques incorporate movement and follow with breathing out the activated energy and consciously breathing in a light vibration such as peace or grace.

Water-Based Techniques

Water is a refreshing and wonderful tool for cleansing and clearing. Water can be used in creative visualization as well, when actual water isn't handy or when you want to get deeper into it.

Washing – The easiest technique of all is to wash your hands or face with plain water, sometimes that isn't enough, so a bath or a shower is better. This refreshes the brain and senses.

Infusions – Adding essential oils to your bath is a common infusion water technique. Placing a crystal in some water and letting it sit for a couple of days can infuse the water with the qualities of the crystals and thereby assist with your clearing work. Salt is a great natural cleanser; you can add it into your water to boost its clearing abilities. You can also explore solar and lunar infusions. Simply put water in a container and leave it in the sunlight or moonlight for what you feel is the right amount of time.

Fire-Based Techniques

Fire can be the most clearing ally. You can incorporate fire in your energy-cleansing work through burning things such as candles, water, through visualizations. It is so powerful that it can actually be dangerous, so always be careful and sensible.

Burning – You can easily write down the energy you want to release on a small piece of paper. Using a set of tongs, hold the paper with the tongs and light it using a long-nosed lighter or a candle. You have to make sure it burns completely, you can then bury the ashes, keep them, or throw them away.

Candle Work – Another method of fire cleansing is to burn a small candle and then try putting all of the energy you want to be released into the candle. To do this you should hold the candle in your hands, center yourself and focus on cleansing negative energy. Once you have released your energy into the candle, you then burn it until it is gone.

Visual Meditation – Visual meditation with fire is a very powerful way to incorporate this tool into your cleansing repertoire. After getting comfortable in your meditative state, practice deep inhaling for a few counts and visualize the breaths as drawing the negative energy and then releasing it.

Air-Based Techniques

Breath Work – for cleansing with air, breathe work is incredible and highly recommended. No tools are required, and it can be done from practically anywhere we are focusing on clearing negative energy, the key is to empty yourself and create space. This means that while you want to take long, slow, deep inhales, the focus is on tor exhale and the release of energy.

Organization – This air technique is especially helpful for clearing the mental energy body and for those who feel overwhelmed by their work life. While it is normal for people to be "At work" all the time, we know it isn't healthy and does not increase productivity, even if it feels like it does. Before you shut down for your weekend, try clearing your emails, your desktop, and maybe even your actual desktop. Crazy, right? The benefits are amazing, you can leave with a clear mind and come back ready for your work week. You can also do things like keep your home more organized, your phone, maybe even keep up more so with things that relate to your health.

Maintain a healthy energetic life is always a work in progress. The nice thing is that once you establish a system and practice it consistently, it eventually becomes second nature, so you can move on to the next area without feeling overwhelmed. Organization and energy clearing work wonders in both the physical and energetic worlds.

Earth-Based Techniques

Crystals – The simplest and most common practice is to carry a crystal around with you so you can touch it whenever you need grounding or earth healing energy.

Trees – Even though it has become somewhat of a joke over the years, hugging trees or leaning against them is such a powerful way to cleanse negative energy. A tree feels so powerful and wise. No matter how chaotic or reactive the energy, I know a tree can handle it. Likewise, even just going outside and touching the ground works if you don't have access to a tree.

Pets – Holding, stroking, or playing with a pet is very calming. Interact with a pet to settle energy, calm your nerves, or brighten your mood.

Napping – This practice may not seem like energy work, but it is among the most effective technique's known: take a nap. When the energy of the mental or emotional bodies are worked up, sometimes being conscious is counterproductive. Sleeping is an effective way to give the mind and emotions space to calm down.

Spiritual-Based Techniques

Spirit-based practices are ideal for contemplative types of people or those who like a more devotional experience with their energy work. Some of the most popular spirit-driven techniques include prayer and good works.

Prayer – or communication with the Divine–can be a simple and direct method of managing energy. For those that have already had prayer practice, this is a natural and easy method. For those who do not pray, it can become a simple, quiet, and beautiful experience if it suits your belief system. In prayer, we commune with the Divine, while meditation is a way to connect with our highest inner wisdom.

Good Works – While it may seem odd to combine spirit-based approaches with mundane physical-world actions, this is a powerful technique. If you know the nature of the energy you want to clear, determine an act that counters it. While most of the practices explained above are great for in-the-moment energy experiences, this one is particularly good for chipping away at long-standing, deep-seated energy within yourself. Sometimes energy takes up residence in us and shapes our behavior in ways that are not consistent with our values. While we would like a single ritual or one healing session to solve all of our issues, that generally doesn't work because those behaviors have become habits. Even if the energy has been released from the energy body through spiritual cleansing practices and healing work, the physical body has to catch up and that takes time for the body to release old habits. Consciously training yourself ends up being a process.

Other Ways to Remove Negative Energy from Home and Body:

- Sweep and clean a lot to get rid of dust, which over time collects energy.
- Essential oils
- Workout to release toxins from the pours
- Sea salt cleanse
- Hanging out with friends

Essential Oils

Essential oils are amazing when used to relax the body and mind. They have been scientifically shown to enter the bloodstream via the lungs and absorb directly into the brain.

Energizing Oils:

- Eucalyptus, Peppermint, Grapefruit, Basil, Wild Orange, Rosemary.

Uplifting oils:

- Peppermint, Bergamot, Geranium, Melissa, Lemon, Wild Orange

Relaxing oils:

- Lavender, Ylang Ylang, Roman Chamomile, Lemon, Geranium.

Sedative oils:

- Lavender, Veviter, Ylang Ylang, Melissa, Geranium, Frankincense.

CHAPTER 4
Incorporating Crystals And Their Knowledge Into Your Daily Life

Harness the positive vibration from healing crystals:

When used properly and with deep respect, crystals can assist you to live an additionally lively and aligned life. Although they are also exceptionally powerful, they are attractive to look at and have a very special significance behind them. You can find crystals practically anywhere these days but I highly encourage visiting a small, local shop. Ask questions about the crystals to make sure they are genuine, they absorb the energy from your extraction to your hands throughout the process, so it matters.

How long does crystal healing take?
Depending on the patient and their states, crystal healing works differently. While it is advisable for other people to undergo crystal healing on a weekly basis to see pain and pressure relief, some people only have to undergo one session.

What crystals can heal
In truth, crystals don't cause direct healing. They won't cure you directly of a disease. Rather, they vibrate with energy your body occupies and then absorbs, and it is you who does the healing by drawing in that energy and communicating with the crystal. Crystals can assist with healing a lot of things, here are some examples:

Body – Your body is your physical side. Crystal can help balance body energy and make physical improvements. These could include things such as relieving low energy and exhaustion, headaches and similar physical problems.

Mind – Your mind is physical as well as immaterial. The vibration in the crystals can help balance the mind's energies to heal. Conditions that can be alleviated include stress, emotional problems, sleeplessness, nightmares, anxiety, depression, grief and lack of enthusiasm.

Spirit – your spirit is the part of you that is completely nonphysical. Crystals assist in balancing spiritual energies such as beliefs, forgiveness, compassion, and unconditional love. They can also facilitate communication with your higher self or higher power.

How to incorporate them into your everyday life
Not all crystal routines are designed for everyone, there are countless ways to work with these fascinating stones, which is why it is important to find out what works best for you. Here are a few ways.

Hold a crystal during meditation
They can give you the energy to guide you in different ways through your meditation.

Create a crystal grid
A specialized pattern of stones used by healers to combine the powers of crystals and their intellectual capacity to strengthen them. You can set your crystals on a grid and symmetrically arrange them. Choose stones that complement your intentions and then the crystals work.

Grid shapes:
Spiral – represents the path to consciousness.
Circles – representation of oneness and unity.
Squares – represent earthly elements.
Triangles – represent the connection between mind body and spirit.

Before you create a crystal grid, you need to contemplate what your intentions for making the grid are. You can either state your intention out loud while creating your grid or alternatively write it down on a piece of paper so you are focused. The intention could be anything you hope for or dream of, such as health, love, fertility, clarity, or focus.

What crystal to use? The first crystal you need to choose is the center stone, also called the master crystal. This crystal is the one that will communicate between the other crystals in the grin. It needs to hold a lot of energy, and some people prefer to use a cluster or pyramid crystals for this placement. The next crystal to choose will be what is called the "activation wand" this will be the crystal to focus your intention on. It is helpful for this crystal to be the same type of crystal as one of the others on the grid. If you want to do long distance healing, either for someone else or a place, you can write the name on a piece of paper and place it on the grid beneath the master crystal.

The rest of the crystals you choose to use will depend on the intention you are focusing on. For example, if your intention is love and romance, use the crystals that match these emotions and thoughts. Alternatively, you can use a pendulum to help you choose the right crystals or simply listen to your own intuition and pick those you feel you should choose. Some people prefer to place clear quartz on the outer points of the grid for the amplification of energy.

Where do you put your grid?
You want to place your grid in an area of your home where it won't be bothered. This could be a quiet corner of a room, or if you have a meditation setup or a sacred place in your home, these are all good places for your grid. Some even believe that placing your grid on the northern side of the room makes the energy stronger, but this is not necessary.

How do you activate the grid?
Once your grid is set up with crystals of your choice, it is time to activate the grid. Here is a guide on how to do this:

1.) Meditate or relax for 5 minutes so you can have reground yourself.
2.) Take hold of the wand, then start your intention or positive affirmation, remembering to focus strongly on what you want the outcome to be.

3.) Now take a moment to accept that your intention is true, called 'programming.'

4.) Wait for a few minutes, then put down your wand and the grid will be activated.

What to do next?

Make sure you take some time each week to sit in front of your grid and simply relax or even better meditate, still focusing on your original intention. You can leave your grid the way it is for weeks at a time, but if you feel like it is losing its strength, you can always recharge it. Simply perform a new activation to recharge the crystals and their energy.

Using crystals for stress.

When your body is experiencing high levels of stress, its natural defenses are weakened, making you more vulnerable to developing physical, mental, and emotional illnesses. Thus stress reduction plays an important role in preserving your wellness and prolonging your life.

Stress reliever crystal pattern for the chakras:
You know where the chakras are located now, so it should be easy for you to follow this method.
What you will need:

- 4 Clear Quartz
- 3 Amethyst
- 2 Black Onyx
- 1 Rose Quartz
- assume a comfortable lying position
- First, lay one Amethyst on your Third Eye Chakra. One Amethyst should be on your right-hand palm while the other should be on your left-hand palm. Its purpose is to ground and calm you. Furthermore, the positioning of these stones is essential to let the energy guide through you.
- Next place one onyx on the sole of your right foot, and another on the sole of your left. The purpose of this is to take

- away and release the negative energies from your body that are responsible for causing stress.
- Place the Rose Quartz on your abdomen. You need to do this to maintain a balance between the female and male energies that all of us possess. Also, place one of the clear Quartz on your abdomen just above the Rose Quartz.
- The second Quartz should be laid above your head. Place the third beside your arm on the right side. The purpose of these clear Quartz crystals is for aura detoxification and chakra cleansing.
- When you're done, you would've successfully created dual triangle energy zones with the positioning of stones.
- Relax your muscles. Close your eyes. Concentrate on your breathing.
- Remain in a meditative state for at least 10 minutes or as long as you need.
- When you are done, you can use the crystals as worry stones. Carry them with you and whenever you feel familiar symptoms of anxiety creeping up, just massage the stones to draw strength from them.

Wear a protection stone.

Crystal amulets have been used and worn for over 30,000 years. More than just accessories or bodily embellishments, amulets serve the purpose of protection, keeping its wearer safe from a variety of dangers depending on the properties of the stone used for the amulet. Back in ancient times, amulets were used as protection against witchcraft, magic spells, and other metaphysical dangers that could be used and enacted by powerful mystics. These days, however, amulets are used for more passive forms of risk, which may be present in a variety of situations. Wearing a protective amulet can keep the wearer safe against situations like these.

When you feel weak against the negative energy, find a quiet space, hold your stone and realign your focus by repeating the intention to yourself. This recharges the energy of the stone and strengthens your defense against negative vibes. The more you have contact with a crystal, the more mindful you are of its energy and healing abilities. The crystal can also be used as a reminder, of any intentions, plans, etc.

Creating a protection shield.
A protection shield can be made from anywhere and works to neutralize negative energy in a space. They work like grids, the only difference is that they use protective stones and work off of a protective intention.

The best crystals for protection are Black Tourmaline, Black Kyanite, Black Onyx, and Pyrite because they are all known for their potent absorbing capabilities relating to their color. They are able to detect negative energy and store it away in their expansive programmable memories. These stones are also known to create protective barriers around a space, perfect for deflecting negative energies.

Placing the crystals on your body.
The placing of crystals on your body has a completely different effect than just holding them. Crystals correspond with chakras so you should keep that in mind when placing them on your body. This helps to stimulate the energy around every chakra and raises the emotions you need to heal.

Sleeping with crystals underneath your pillow.
This is highly advised if you are suffering from insomnia or night terrors. Keeping crystals underneath your pillow will enable you to feel more revitalized upon waking up. To ward of bad dreams, use hematite, ruby, or Smoky Quartz.

Place Aventurine over your heart to open the heart chakra for love. Smoky quartz to give your root chakra some grounding energy and place Quartz above your head to enlighten and guide your crown chakra.

Why do Crystals Work?
Because of the structure of a crystal, they are able to absorb, focus, and transmit subtle electromagnetic energy. This is the energy used in healing/gem therapy. Clear quartz is proven to of been on this earth since the beginning of time, ancient civilizations have

used crystals as protecting talismans, peace offerings, and quite often jewelry. Quarts makes up 12 percent of the earth's crust and is used in almost all technology. Involves timekeeping, electronics, storage of information and more. If it is possible for crystals to communicate through computer chips, then isn't it possible that this vibrational energy could be transformed in other ways? And with their connection to the earth and its life-giving elements. It makes sense that crystals are universally healing, especially since they've made their mark in almost every civilization before us.

One of the first pieces of scientific evidence relating to the power of crystals is the work done by IBM scientist Marcel Vogel. While watching crystals grow under a microscope, he noticed that their shape took the form of whatever he thought. He assumed that these vibrations resulted from the constant assembly and disassembly of bonds between molecules. He also often tested the metaphysical power of quartz crystal and demonstrated that rocks can store ideas similar to how tapes use magnetic energy to track sound.

At every moment, we have the ability to choose our thoughts as we continue our journey, each day presents us with new challenges and wonderful beginnings. Healing crystals remind us to quiet the chatter of the mind and reconnect to the universally healing vibrations of the earth. You must be patient with crystals because just like all eons of time it took for these semi-precious stones to evolve and transform, working with the healing powers of crystals also takes time. As you deepen your knowledge and evolve, use crystals as a reminder to be grateful for the abundance of Mother Nature and the great mysteries of the universe.

Maintenance of Your Crystals

When you first get a crystal, no matter where it came from, it is always a good idea to cleanse it before use. Crystals are great at absorbing energy, which is the property used to protect you from negative influences. They can get full though, and when that happens, they must be cleansed in order to work at their maximum potential.

Cleansing the crystal

Leave it buried in sea salt overnight, on a clear and empty tabletop. The salt will absorb the impurities locked within the crystal, leaving it fresh and ready to protect you from negative energy.

Recharging the crystal
You have a few ways to go about recharging your crystal.

Direct sun or moonlight – Your first option is to leave the crystal in direct sun or moonlight, this will recharge the stones and bring them back to their original configuration.

Burying – you can also bury the stone in the ground to let it reclaim the healing powers of the earth. You can also submerge the crystals in dry brown rice or sand, they are both absorbent. It should only take a day or two to recharge crystals this way.

Meditate – You may also meditate with the crystal, directing your thoughts, needs, and desires into it with deep, forceful breaths.

Clear Quartz – One of the crystals functions is to cleanse other crystals, which gives it a unique position in your set. A clean clear quartz can be used to recharge other crystals in your arsenal as they vibrate purifying energy that neutralizes negative energy in surrounding stones.

Programming Your Crystal

To become more in-tune with your crystals energy emissions, you should spend some time getting to know them. You can program your crystals by telling them visualizations while talking to them. Many healers program their crystals to person-specific healing functions for their practices. You must ensure that your jewel is in harmony with your programming purpose.

Any type of crystal programming is a way to sort a stone's energy design. The programmed energy pattern in the jewel can be an idea, intention, sound, color, emotion, or other oscillations. These vibrations are often used to redirect the energy of your main motive. Here are the top tips that you should not miss if you need to program your crystals:

Clear your crystals – You must make them lucid, whatever kind of crystals and approaches you prefer. Sit at your altar, which is designed for you, while holding your crystals. Make sure the programming of your crystal is done with no interferences.

Hold your crystals firmly – Use your right hand to hold your crystals and to clear your unrelated ideas. Start focusing on your goal of successful crystal programming.

Focus your intention – You must concentrate on your objective while programming. This can be done by saying loud and clear illustrative words. For example, if you choose to program your crystals for good health, repeat the phrase " good health" over and over again.

Repeat your purpose verbally – Make sure you hold your crystals and repeat your goal. Never leave your crystals for programming. You should also stretch your hand over the crystals to produce more energy.

Keep holding your crystals – Repeat the steps for a few times as much as you can. Open your hand slowly when your instinct tells you that the crystals have absorbed the energies, then thank you for your crystals.

Following these procedures, your crystals are fully programmed. This process can also be used with words, tumbled rocks, polished crystals, natural crystals, and minerals.

How to Tell Apart Real and Fake

There are countless crystal shops out there that are genuinely interested in providing you with good quality crystals and there are just as many unscrupulous sellers who simply live and build on the rebirth of crystal healing. Here are some ways you can tell real crystals apart from fakes:

- **Bubbles** – Crystals are formed through a variety of processes in the presence of a number of different elements and conditions. In all cases, crystals are formed entirely solid – with no room for air to form bubbles. If you inspect your crystal up close and find bubbles it is most likely not made out of naturally occurring elements.

- ***Unnatural Rich colors*** – Fraudulent sellers will often exaggerate colors to make them more appealing to the eye. Remember, natural crystals are formed in the earth, typically with a range of tinged earthy tones that might dampen their otherwise vibrant colors. Crystals that are too richly hued, and seem to not have any trace of earth on their surface, is likely to be a hoax.

- ***Magnification*** – in this case of clear crystals such as quartz, you can easily check for magnification. As a general rule, crystals shouldn't' magnify any objects in their background. Therefore, if you place a questionable stone on the page of a book and the works are enlarged when you look through the crystal, its likely made of glass.

- ***Perfect Surfaces*** – while crystals can be chiseled and shaped to make them look more aesthetically pleasing, there is no such thing as a perfect crystal, as objects born raw from the earth, even with all the buffing and shaping wouldn't be able to clear away layers of impurities. Most crystals will have traces of earth, cracks, and discoloration throughout its surfaces.

The color of a crystal can actually affect how attractive it is to you, but the color also plays a role in the energetic and healing impacts of crystals. The color of the crystal comes from three things:

- How the crystal absorbs light?

- The specific minerals/chemicals the crystal contains

- Any impurities within the crystal

The Six Crystal Lattice Patterns

Hexagonal – crystals have an interior structure that resembles a 3-D hexagon. Hexagonal crystals help with manifestation.

Isometric – crystals have an interior cubic structure. These crystals can improve situations and amplify energies.

Monoclinic – these crystals have a 3-D parallelogram structure. They are protective crystals.

Orthorhombic – these crystals have a diamond-shaped crystalline pattern. They cleanse, clear, and remove blockages.

Tetragonal – these crystals have a rectangular interior structure. These crystals are attractors; they make things more attractive and they help attract things to you.

Triclinic – these crystals have an interior structure with three inclines axes. These crystals ward off unwanted energies and help retain energies you'd like to keep

The minerals and impurities impact which light wavelengths the crystal will absorb and the color that appears as a result. For example, if a crystal absorbs all of the light wavelengths, it appears black. If it doesn't absorb any light wavelengths, it appears clear. Different impurities and chemicals/minerals affect light differently.

Crystals, Gems, Minerals, or Rocks?

It may seem as though people use the terms crystal, gem, mineral, and rock interchangeably, which is common when discussing crystals. In fact, some substances that aren't crystals, such as amber (petrified tree sap), are also referred to as crystals or stones. However, here's a quick overview:

Crystal – a mineral that has a crystalline interior structure. Agate, which is a hexagonal crystal, is also a mineral and rock.

Gem – a cut and polished crystal, mineral, or rock, a cut diamond (which is mineral, crystal, and rock) is also a gem or gemstone. Amber and pearls are organic substances that are considered gemstones, but they are not crystals, minerals, or rocks.

Mineral – A naturally occurring substance with a particular chemical composition and a highly ordered structure, crystalline or not. Opal is a mineral that does not have a crystalline structure; it's a gemstone and a rock but not a true crystal.

Rock – a combination, or aggregate, of minerals. Marble, which is made up of multiple minerals, is a metamorphic rock – a rock that has been subjected to heat and pressure over time.

Crystal Shapes

Obelisks – There are four-sided pillars forming in a pyramid shape. Symbolically, an obelisk can release tension through its tip and send it into the dissipated atmosphere. It can also draw energy from the higher atmosphere and base this energy.

Pyramids – Can be used to concentrate and base energy. They can also absorb negative energy and help all of the chakras. A gemstone pyramid is also used to enhance and concentrate the inherent properties of the stone.

Spheres / Crystal Balls – symbolize the cyclical nature of life. Circles symbolize infinity because they have no beginning and no end. Spheres/balls are usually used for healing and rituals.

Tumbled Stones – It has no rough edges and is convenient for healing or grid work. In addition, they are convenient to carry.

Crystal Clusters – Brings harmony. Clusters like Quartz crystal clusters were used to meditate, heal and expand the mind to touch the spiritual world.

Different Types of Minerals

Igneous – It is formed by magma or lava cooling and solidification.

Sedimentary – formed through the accumulation of sediments of other rocks, usually in seas and oceans or in the Grand Canyon.

Metamorphic – formed when rocks were forced to change their shape and composition due to exposure to tremendous heat or pressure.

What is the different between a crystal and a mineral?

Have you ever wondered what the real difference between crystals and minerals is? Many people say that they are the same. If you think the same way, you are wrong. There are important differences between the two and you can distinguish them from person to person.

Minerals are regarded as one of the world's most important natural resources. They are found in solid chemicals and often formed through many geological processes. Most of them have a very diverse make-up compound. They are highly ordered atomic formations with explicit physical properties.

The composition of minerals varies from simple salts to complex silicates. Minerals are used differently, most of which are either grown or owned. Crystals, on the other hand, consist of ions, molecules, and atoms that are arranged in a repeated outline that recognizes all three spatial dimensions. The mineral composition varies between simple salts and complex silicates. Minerals are used differently, most of them either cultivated or owned. On the other hand, crystals consist of ions, molecules, and atoms that are arranged in a repeated outline that recognizes all three dimensions of space.

Minerals Vs. Crystals

Minerals and crystals are not only different in the manner in which they are utilized. They also differ in terms of creation. Simply put, crystals consist of several natural materials. Crystals are classified as cubic, monoclinic, orthorhombic, hexagonal and tetragonal forms. They are also used in various relaxation processes and are believed to have healing properties.

Crystals are not dark in color and have translucent features. Some of these reflect light in a variety of colors. Based on the structure and the rare characteristics of the crystals, some are cheap while others are not. In addition, minerals are divided into two groups, silicates, and non-silicates. Silicate minerals are materials which have a basic silicate mineral unit.

On the flip side, the non-silicates are divided into several categories, such as Elements, Hydroxides, Carbonates, and Sulphides. Non-silicate minerals are quite rare than many of the other type's.

What is the best crystal?
Since many types of healing crystals are present, you must choose the right one. Not all crystals are created evenly. If you want these crystals, please consult first the experts. Some healers say that some crystals have extraordinary effects on the digestive system, although some are necessary for the reproductive system to be restored.

Whatever kind of problem you may have; a similar healing crystal suits your condition. Do not forget to consider the information provided above in the event you do not know. You can also ask some friends what you need and treat your condition instantly.

Do's and Don'ts with Crystals

Do not wear crystals immediately after purchase. Make sure you follow their programming approach, which will clean them up. Cleanse may vary from running water to being soaked overnight. Always ask the seller before wearing crystals for the best way to eliminate depression and energy.

Don't be distressed if your stones fall, crack, break or get lost. Most crystal healers believe their work is done after it has been bought.

Do get your crystals into power. You can do this by asking a healer or an astrologer for help. This can help crystals or gemstones to function on their own for the user.

Always trust the feeling in your gut about crystals. If you think your favorite stones are working efficiently and ideal, get them. Leave them if you feel uncertain about them.

CHAPTER 5
Starting A Crystal Collection

Choosing a Crystal for Yourself

Make sure you are well educated on each of the crystals you collect. The best way to choose a crystal is to feel its energy. Trust your intuition and your sense of what feels right to you. Let yourself be guided to the crystal, so let it choose you.

There is a wide range of experiences that crystal shoppers report when choosing a crystal. Often, I personally feel a good vibe and a slight tingling sensation.

- Heat emitting from stone
- A dash of light from the crystal
- Cold energy
- Lightheaded sensation
- Ringing Ears
- Sudden rush of excitement

You should also take note of crystals that you feel you dislike. More often then not they represent qualities or issues you need to deal with.

Choose By Crystal System

Each crystal is part of a different crystal system with specific properties. The crystal systems include:

Hexagonal crystals, which manifest

Isometric crystals, which improve situations and amplify energies

Monoclinic crystals, which protect and safeguard

Orthorhombic crystals, which cleanse, clear, unblock, and release

Tetragonal crystals, which contain or ward off energies

Amorphous "crystals," which have differing properties.

Choosing By Color

The importance of color extends far beyond personal preference. Each color has its own vibrational energies with associated healing properties. By choosing a crystal of the crystal system that has the properties you'd like it to display along with the healing principles of the color, you can select crystals quite specifically for certain conditions.

Choose By How They Make You Feel

When you choose a crystal, you should hold it in your hand and see how it makes you feel. Note whether or not they make you feel comfortable or uncomfortable if they feel heavy or light, and if you feel other sensations. You should feel a pleasant feeling.

Pairing Crystals

Like wine and cheese, some crystals pair well to make them better than the sum of their parts. Crystals that pair well have complementary energies that can really help focus energy. For example, the energy of any crystal is amplified when paired with clear quartz. Here are some other pairings that work well:

Smoky Quartz and Apache Tears – a powerful combination for people who are grieving.
Amethyst and Labradorite – can help you get a more restful nights' sleep.
Citrine and Black Tourmaline – can help ground you in prosperity.
Rose Quartz and Ruby or Garnet – excellent for pairing relationships
Black Tourmaline and Clear Quartz – help facilitate the free flow of balanced energy.

Choose By Using a Dowsing Rod

considered to be a more advanced process, but beginners can effectively learn how to use one in order to discover the best stones for their initial practice. Keep in mind though that pendulum dowsing might require a higher level of intuition.

As one of the oldest forms of divination, pendulum dowsing allows us to discover the energy of crystals, guiding us towards the one that is most attuned to our spirit. Of course in the process of finding a pendulum, it is important that you find the right one for you to help guarantee a seamless and effective experience.

To choose a pendulum, observe a selection of them. Your spirit will know what is best for you and will gravitate you towards the right one without you having to exert any cognitive effort. Once you have a pendulum, you can start using it to choose crystals, ask it questions, or it can assist you in making decisions that result in a yes or no answer.

Steps in using a pendulum dowser for crystal selection:
Clear your mind – Before starting any of kind of process with crystals, it's important that your mind is clear from possible distractions. Take a few minutes to focus on your breathing and set your mind to the goal of the dowsing experience.

Practice Your Pendulum

Different pendulums vibrate with different intensity and quality. So what feels like a 'yes' with one pendulum, might feel completely different with another. To attune to your specific pendulum, hold it in your hand and close your eyes. Ask it a question to which you know the answer will be yes. Once you've felt the vibrations of a yes answer, ask it a question whose answer would be no. you should be able to sense a change in the vibration of your pendulum. In doing this, you develop a deeper sense of your pendulum, thus allowing you to better understand where it wants to guide you.

Choose your crystals – When using a pendulum dowser to select crystals, simply hold the pendulum over the crystal, or over an image of the crystal if you're buying it online, and ask it a question referring to the crystal. Try not to make suggestions in your mind to influence the answer of the pendulum as this could interfere with its true recommending. Try to maintain an open mind.

Where to Shop

There are many sources where you can purchase stones –both in brick-and-mortar stores and online. Many towns and cities have retail crystal outlets. These may be listed as metaphysical bookshops, crystal stores, or New Age shops. With knowledgeable staff, most will let you handle the crystals before you purchase. You can also find traveling mineral or gem shows are a great place to purchase crystals and can't be beaten for selection or price. Although these usually need to be planned for in advance. You can even buy crystals online when making a purchase ensure that you're working with a reliable seller. You may want to use your pendulum when ordering crystals online.

Crystal Starter Kit

Clear Quartz – if you don't know which crystal to use, start with clear quartz; it works with every type of energy.

Smoky Quartz – is the crystals a lot of people use because it's a manifestation stone that converts negative energy into positive.

Citrine – promotes self-esteem and prosperity

Rose Quartz – supports all types of love, including unconditional and romantic love.

Amethyst – helps you tune into intuition and guidance from higher realms, as well as the power of your dreams

Black Tourmaline – is a grounding stone that is protective and that keeps negativity at bay.

Rainbow Fluorite – deepens intuition, promotes love, and facilitates clear communication.

Carnelian – helps you set appropriate boundaries, have integrity, and be creative.

Hematite – is protective, grounding, and centering and can also attract energies you'd like into your life.

Turquoise – promotes good luck, prosperity, and personal power.

Sacred Geometry of Cut Stones

You can find crystals cut into many different shapes, including spheres and polyhedrons, which have varying properties. Working with stones cut into these shapes will impart the properties of both the crystal and the sacred shape.

Dodecahedron – the dodecahedron is associated with the element of the Ethereal realm and connects you to intuition and higher realms.

Hexahedron – the hexahedron, or cube, represents the element of earth. It is grounding and stable.

Icosahedron – the icosahedron is linked to the element of water. It connects you to change and flow.

Merkaba – the Merkaba is a 3-D star. It contains all five of the above polyhedrons within it and therefore combines all the effects of each. It is also associated with the energy of sacred truth and eternal wisdom.

Octahedron – the octahedron represents the element of Air and promotes compassion, kindness, forgiveness, and love.

Sphere – the sphere has the energy of completeness, wholeness, and oneness.

Tetrahedron – associated with the element of fire, a tetrahedron promotes balance, stability, and the ability to create change.

Other Names for Crystals

In recent years, some retailers have given brand names to crystals and have in some cases marked them. The reason they are typically branded is usually because it originates from a particular area on property owned by the people who brand it, but the location does not greatly affect the properties of the crystal.

- Amazon Jade is Amazonite.
- Aqua Terra Jasper is either resin or onyx.
- Atlantis Stone is Larimar.
- Azeztulite is and has the same properties as clear quartz.
- Boji stones can also be found non-branded as Kansas pop rocks.
- Healerite is generically found as Chrysolite.
- Isis Calcite is the branded form of white calcite.
- Lemurian Light Crystals are a branded form of Lemurian quartz.
- Mani Stone is black-and-white jasper.
- Master Shamanite is the same as black calcite.
- Merkabite Calcite is white Calcite
- Revelation Stone is brown or red jasper.
- Sauralite Azeztuline is quartz from New Zealand.
- Zultanite is the mineral diaspore.
- Agape Crystals are a combination of seven different crystals: clear quartz, smoky quartz, rusticated quarts, amethyst, goethite, lepidocrocite, and cacoxenite.

Crystal Safety

In general, working with crystals is relatively safe. However, some crystals contain substances (such as aluminum, copper, sulfur, fluorine, strontium, or asbestos) that are toxic to humans, so do not put them in the bathtub or make a crystal elixir with them. It's also best to wash your hands when you've finished holding them. These crystals include:

- Aquamarine (contains aluminum)
- Black Tourmaline (contains aluminum)
- Celestite (contains strontium)
- Cinnabar (contains mercury)
- Dioptase (contains copper)
- Emerald (contains aluminum)
- Fluorite (contains fluorine)
- Garnet (contains aluminum)
- Iolite (contains aluminum)
- Jade (contains asbestos)
- Kansas pop rocks (contains aluminum)
- Labradorite (contains aluminum)
- Lapis lazuli (contains pyrite, which contains sulfur)
- Malachite (contains copper)
- Moldavite (contains aluminum)
- Moonstone (contains aluminum)
- Prehnite (contains aluminum)
- Ruby (contains aluminum)
- Sapphire (contains aluminum)
- Sodalite (contains aluminum)
- Spinel (contains aluminum)

- Sugilite (contains aluminum)
- Sulfur (contains poisonous)
- Tanzanite (contains aluminum)
- Tigers eye, unpolished (contains asbestos)
- Topaz (contains aluminum)
- Tourmaline (contains aluminum)
- Turquoise (contains aluminum)
- Zircon (contains zirconium)

CHAPTER 6
Different Types Of Energy Healing

Energy Healing

Everything starts with energy. "If you want to find the secrets of the universe, think about energy, frequency, and vibration," says physicist Nikola Tesla. Energy is the one thing which can be changed but never destroyed. Energy is where the secrets of healing of crystals lie.

Indigenous cultures have had a positive influence on the health of the body for thousands of years by working with its energy fields, otherwise known as Chakras. Reiki is a Japanese tradition from the beginning of the 20th century, chakras are vividly described in ancient Hindu texts, and traditional Chinese practitioners studied meridians. Many people around the world even talk about how medical practices use the techniques related to crystals. Although almost every culture had a different idea of stimulating the ability of the body to heal itself, a positive force of good was how everyone viewed internal energy.

How it Works
Energy healing flows directly into the wavelength with the spiritual, emotional, and physical characteristics of our beings. It dispatches upsets in your flow of energy. The body stays balanced and healthy when the energy fields and flow are vibrant and equal.

Energy healing is actually based on scientific principles
As you may know, everything is constantly vibrating, always. We, humans, vibrate too. When somebody is referring to a "good vibe" they are really talking about the personal vibrational energy, the one that each and every one of us emits. Even places have vibrational frequencies. Have you ever walked into a new room and felt the energy change?

You don't have to be spiritual to benefit from energy healing

Just like you don't have to know somebody to feel like you know them. You don't need to know everything about healing energy before you start, all you need is an open mind for the maximum benefit.

You can maintain your energetic health at home
Once you have visited an energy healer or performed an energy healing process, it is important that you keep the positive energy streaming by meditating, burning sage, taking a bath, or choosing essential oils. Even having your own crystals is always a good way to keep the good vibrations flowing.

It is always a great time to pull the crystals out or to visit an energy healer. Even if you feel anxious or drained by the day, a session will aid you to feel more balanced and relax.

Energy healing is very accessible
Healers of energy come in numerous types. They are all over the world and there are usually some in your city.

Reiki – Uses the chi energy to strengthen and help people use specific symbols and hand techniques to heal their bodies by channeling the universe's energy. Master teachers who train you for long periods of time can only teach you. Practitioners actually settle throughout the world, one fascinating thing about Reiki healing is that you don't have to be in the same place as the practitioner since the power of intention does not cause energy to flow where it is needed the most.

Acupuncture – By the insertion of needles through the skin at certain high energy points in the body, it stimulates your body's energy flow. The meridians are targeted to bring back equilibrium. It is often done to reduce chronic back pain, neck pain, and knees. Although customers also need to be in the physical presence of the needles, practitioners are very accessible. This kind of treatment stimulates the flow of the chi to equilibrate the body.

Even ***Massage*** is an energy healing, releasing built up tension in the muscles, encouraging the flow of deep relaxation.

More Energy Healing Techniques Are

Crystal Medicine
The use of crystals and stones to remove contaminants in the body. These stones have specific properties that aim at various types of problems with spiritual, physical, and emotional energy. Aligning stones on the body's chakra points are what most crystal healers do, keeping in mind the symptoms reported by the person being treated.

Quantum Healing
A natural healing method combined with the body's life energy to promote optimum well-being. Quantum mechanics science is where Quantum healing is based on. It delves into how frequencies and quantum affects the body and teaches us how to control, amplify, focus, and project this energy, which emerges in a wide range of advantages with extraordinary results.

Elixirs
Elixirs are liquids, usually water, which is combined with properties of a crystal and used to allow you to drink the properties associated with the crystal It is a quick, easy method to receive a healing. You can easily make your own elixir at home.

Qigong
Qigong comes from the word "qi" meaning, "living force" or "energy," and gong means "work" or effort." Qigong cultivates and practices the breathing and meditation techniques of vital life force. Medical Qigong has two types: self-healing Qigong, in which you use Qigong exercises to prevent diseases, improve your health and treat disease, while external Qigong or qi emissions emit qi in order to cure others.

Spiritual Healing
This type of healing is a mixture of physical, medical, and non-medical, energetic interventions and mental interventions. When we are transforming the cause of illness/disease and learn to grow beyond the problem, we are then focused on healing ourselves.

In spiritual healing, we create a medicine story for ourselves that includes both a curing process and a healing destination. When embarking on a spiritual healing journey, you are to address physical, emotional, mental, and spiritual toxins. Healing the soul takes combines healing interventions for the heart, body, and mind.

Spiritual Healing Techniques

- *Exercise.* Find an exercise you enjoy and can integrate into your daily life.

- *Eat healthily.* Eat more vegetable! Learn about your diet and eat more local organics.

- *Care for your body.* Pay attention to your body, do things that help you relax or go visit a healer.

- *Sleep.* Make sure you are getting the appropriate amount of sleep. Try to hit the hay earlier, sleep deprivation can cause serious imbalances in the human body. Mentally and physically.

What kind of change can you expect?
When we do energy work, the energy always seeks to align with our highest and greatest good. Sometimes the change you think you need isn't what best serves you. Remove any expectation of the outcome and allow what serves you to arise. When we set expectations and stick to them, we limit results, because what we imagine is usually smaller than what the universe provides. And sometimes what serves our greatest good doesn't appear as we think it should. As much as you can, remove "should" and "could" from your vocabulary and accept what the energy brings.

CHAPTER 7
Types Of Healing Crystals

These are just among some of the most known and powerful healing crystals we have around today. These stones are used for a very large variety of things such as energy healing, meditation, technology, and mainly jewelry. Most people don't have time every day to engage in cleansing with crystals, therefore they wear them around their neck based upon their qualities and healing benefits.

Types of Gemstones

Precious – hard and often made into jewelry. They have a high value because they are of their scarcity, hardness, transparency, color, and brilliance.
Ex: Emerald, Pearl Sapphire.

Semi-Precious – made from a portion of mineral, more common and usually less expensive. These stones are mainly used for making jewelry.
Ex: Agate, Aventurine, Tourmaline.

Ornamental – usually extremely hard to find but not rare. They are used for ornamental value, meaning used in statues, decorations, and personal items.
Ex: Quartz, Lapis lazuli, Jade.

<u>Charoite</u>

The Lilac Stone

- Is always a dark shade of purple, but you will find traces of white, grey, and black on the stone, making it one of the most attractive crystals in the world.
- First discovered in Russia, along the Chara River in the 1940s.

- Excellent for making goblets, vases, or bookends.

Metaphysical Healing Properties:

- This stone can heal the body, the heart, and the spirit. It helps to remove the negativity from your life and protects you against the negative.
- Give you the emotional support you need to consolidate, reflect and re-strategize.
- Charoite will open your heart so that in your life you can clearly see and feel the love. It will break down your walls and throw your fears away.
- It can help to unleash your creativity and encourage you to live a life of truth, it can help to ensure you are working to overcome your fears and live your own life.

Physical Healing Properties:

- Has the power to transmute disease to wellness. It is effective in relieving pain, aches and can help speed up the healing process.
- Known to alleviate arthritis symptoms and to provide rapid relief for headaches, migraines, cramps and other pains and aches.
- Helps to control blood pressure and helps to treat heart-related diseases and conditions.
- Known for body detoxification, especially if you are trying to quit bad habits.

Chakra: Heart Chakra, Root Chakra.

Howlite

Stone of Eternal Wisdom

- Named after the mineralogist who first discovered it in Nova Scotia.
- Creates nodules often that look very much like cauliflower heads.
- Can be found in regions all over the world.

Metaphysical Healing Properties:

- Will give you the gift of wisdom and understanding. Can help you connect to higher realms and eliminate the veils that block the truths in your life.
- Will help you to rid yourself of stress and anxiety because it's a powerful calming stone.
- Can help you to process your emotions so that in all aspects of your life they can give you peace, happiness, and feeling of content.
- Calms your upset or worried state of mind effectively, softens or removes your aggressiveness and allows you to recognize when you are unreasonable.
- Eliminates selfishness and thoughtlessness.
- The energies in this stone can support the healing of various physical and mental states.

Physical Healing Properties:

- It can also act as a pain reliever for cramps and other forms of physical pain if you use it as a gem elixir before going to bed.
- Assistance in the treatment of anxiety disorder and other stress-related diseases has been known.
- Also good for bones and can help with bone-related illnesses or conditions, such as osteoporosis.
- Can balance your calcium levels and help to correctly distribute the nutrients you need.
- Great enhancer of memory and mood stabilizer.

Chakra: Crown Chakra.

Morganite
Stone of Strength

- The pink color of this stone is caused by the presence of magnesium in the stone, and the heat treatments that this stone undergoes enhance the colors as well.
- Discovered in California in the early 1900s.
- Also known as pink emerald.

Metaphysical Healing Properties:

- Will help you realize that your bad experiences and challenges will be the catalyst for moving forward or making that big change in your life.
- Can help you discover your own strength, courage, and it will help give you peace and confidence to just keep going.
- Will make you realize all the things and all the people you have been taking for granted, and it will teach you how you can demonstrate your gratitude for them.
- Assists in giving you peace and quiet during your busy and crazy days can also help you distress.
- Can make you more receptive to gentle and loving words and actions from other people.

Physical Healing Properties:

- Supports the heart and counter heart-related problems, illnesses, and disorders. It can help with heart palpitations.
- Can be used for treating tuberculosis, emphysema, and asthma as well.

- Beneficial for people who suffer from vertigo and is known to help with larynx, thyroid, and tongue problems, too.
- Can assist in clearing the lungs and relieving any kind of stress-related illnesses.

Chakra: Heart Chakra.

Variscite

The True Worry Stone

- Often referred to as Utah-lite for the reason that it is commonly found in Utah, USA.

Metaphysical Healing Properties:

- This stone will help you accept some hard realities regarding yourself, it will help liberate you from your bad habits for you to fully heal and transform.
- Show you how your personal power can be harnessed by converting your weaknesses into strengths and concentrating on your strengths.
- Eliminates fear, anxiety, anxiety, and body tension.
- As easy as having this stone near your personal auric field, you will get that boost of energy, it will replenish your energy supply, inspiration, or motivation.
- Also beneficial to your intuition and psychological perceptions. Great for past life, remember and guide you to the information you seek.

Physical Healing Properties:

- Strengthens the cells and tissues of the body, can also help to treat blood disorders and deal with blood flow problems.
- Abdominal distension, gastritis, ulcer, gout or rheumatism may be treated.

- Neutralizes over acidity and can benefit muscles and kidneys very much.
- Helps in any treatment related to the Skelton and the nervous system.

Chakra: Heart Chakra, Solar Plexus Chakra.

Silicon

The Stone of Element

- Found usually as part of something else.
- Can be found anywhere in the world, and there are wide and varied uses and benefits.
- A pure energy element.

Metaphysical Healing Properties:

- Improves your communication and clearly and positively transmits your thoughts, improves your focus and your mental agility.
- Sharpens your focus and increases your mental activity.
- Silicon energies will help you to decipher the truth from lies.
- Can assist you in identifying facts from a barrage of conflicting information.
- Promotes and enhances positive energies in all situations.

Physical Healing Properties:

- A master healing stone that can help heal headaches. It can also relieve the eye strain caused by overuse of your computer.
- A great booster of vitality to recharge and revitalize the body. Its healing energies can also consolidate teeth and bones.

- Can assist in the correct calcium assimilation for bone and joint maintenance and growth. Ensures good skeletal health for dislocation and fracture prevention.

Chakra: Crown Chakra, Root Chakra.

Merlinite
The Stone of Duality

- Speaks about light properties and dark ones.
- Their vibrations foster spiritual growth.
- Named after the Merlin wizard for the ability of stones to attract mystical and magical experiences to anyone wearing them.
- Only found in New Mexico, USA.

Metaphysical Healing Properties:

- Encourages the harmonization of heavenly and earthly energies.
- This stone will allow you to connect with the world of spirits and allow spirits into your life.
- Will help you become more open and accessible, it will also help you to embrace things that are out of the ordinary or different from your normal ways in your life.
- Working with this stone's energies will boost your creativity and enhance your overall organizational skills.
- Merlinite will enhance your magical and psychic abilities if you access higher levels of consciousness.
- Will also help you balance your masculine and feminine energies to better understand your inner god and goddess.

Physical Healing Properties:

- A powerful aid in the treatment of heart and intestine-related diseases and conditions.
- A known stabilization of the nervous system. It also helps with the circulatory and respiratory systems.
- Used to treat disorders affecting the veins, arteries, and skeletal structures.
- Can promote physical development and better circulation of blood. It is also a powerful cleaning stone, which can improve the lymph flow and excretion of the body.

Chakra: Solar Plexus Chakra, Third-eye Chakra.

Wonderstone

The Stone of Curiosity

- A type of Jasper.
- Wonderful stone for meditation.

Metaphysical Healing Properties:

- Will integrate your past with the present and heal unhealthy past life energies that affect your present, resulting in your total acceptance.
- Wonderstone will help you stay determined, especially when you experience a dry spell on your earnings and jobs.
- Can strengthen your psychic powers and enhance and maintain your channeling connections.
- Used often in psychological contact with your loved ones who have moved to the other side.
- has an incredible ability to channel tote animals and also to access internal wisdom.

Physical Healing Properties:

- Can combat most types of infection, especially from bites of animals and insects. It can also help calm general irritations of the skin.
- Can support the natural resistance of the body, provide physical vitality and muscle tone. It is known to be effective in relieving abdominal pain and back pain.
- The balancing properties of the nervous system and harmonious production can also be regulated with this stone.
- Can clean and clean the liver and enhance the immune system. It can also help people with multiple sclerosis, Parkinson's disease, and sciatica.

Chakra: Solar Plexus Chakra, Root Chakra, Heart Chakra.

Mariposite

Stone of the Night

- This stone comes from California's Mariposa County, and hence its name.
- The Spanish word "Mariposa," meaning butterfly, also derives this name.

Metaphysical Healing Properties:

- Will affect the physical, emotional, mental and spiritual aspects of your life in a positive way. Will also encourage you to be more flexible in your perspective and personality so that you can adapt to new environments and situations more easily and confidently.
- Mariposite may bring you dreams, revelations, and visions prophetic and phenomenal.
- Will help you to align yourselves with higher realms and your life.

- Can help to stimulate self-expression in your creative pursuits, which is why it should be regarded as a power stone for creative and artistic types
- This stone will help you to communicate better with everything in your environment and surroundings.

Physical Healing Properties:

- Can help to alleviate insomnia and sleeping problems.
- Will enhance the reproductive system functions of women.
- It can cure skin diseases and protect the sweat glands and the ovules.

Chakra: Heart Chakra.

Galaxite

The Galaxy Stone

- A micro-labradorite that holds powerful energy.
- The stone has an appearance of a galaxy of stars.
- Discovered in the small town of Galax, Virginia, USA.
- If you find yourself overly drawn to the beauty and energy of Galaxite, it might mean that you are looking for your next great adventure.
- Believed to be sent to earth by the angels

Metaphysical Healing Properties:

- This stone will enhance both your conscious and subconscious mind.
- Assists in contacting the higher realm, your spirit guides, your guardian angels, and even beings from other planes and dimensions.
- Eases stress and anxiety, as well as eliminates worries.

- Particularly helpful in astral projection and astral travel.

Physical Healing Properties:

- Aids with anxiety disorders, and is well known to be helpful with certain brain disorders as well.
- Known to be particularly effective against sinus infections, head colds, and regular colds.
- Can help with problems in digestion and metabolic illnesses.
- Can be used to ease the pains or discomfort that come with menstruation, such as PMS, menstrual cramps, bloating, headaches, or lethargy.

Chakra: Crown Chakra.

Okenite

Stone of the New Age

- Part of the Zeolites family.
- It looks like small white snowballs in some formations
- It is named after a German naturalist and can be found mainly in India.

Metaphysical Healing Properties:

- Supports the manifestation in this world of your higher self-energies.
- A stone that will help clear your way obstacles. If the road is clear and smooth, the possibilities are unlimited.
- Encourage you and others to forgive themselves and experience complete emotional healing.
- Gives you the strength to complete your objectives and tasks. The supporting energies of the stones will encourage

- you to break bad habits and to develop good habits that bring you closer to your objectives.
- This stone will help you to channel your chakras and purify them.

Physical Healing Properties:

- Helps to promote good milk flow for nursing mothers.
- stimulates and improves the circulation of the upper body.
- Can assist with blood and stomach disease treatment.
- This stone helps to balance emotions and hormone changes.

Chakra: Crown Chakra, Solar Plexus Chakra.

Wavellite

The Stone of Perspective

- Named after an English doctor who discovered the stone first.
- Found throughout the world.
- Crystal trade desirability is high for wavellite.

Metaphysical Healing Properties:

- This stone helps you to recognize that everyone is the same and that everyone comes from the same source.
- It will help remind you that it is only gained wisdom by determined observations, which help you conquer new struggles and challenges.
- Will aid you in managing problematic circumstances so that you can understand why these struggles and challenges lie before you.
- Can help you look at a larger picture before taking a decision or taking action.

- It has a very simple vibration and each new moon it grows more powerful. It develops your psychological skills and strengthens your intuition.

Physical Healing Properties:

- Used to treat dermatitis, blood flow increases, and stabilizes the blood count.
- Known also to clear any "cellular memory" that might otherwise have disease states induced.
- Wavellite is considered a great "energy flow balancer" that acts as a regulator for peak physical health.
- used in flow treatment (energy, blood)

Chakra: Heart Chakra, Third-eye Chakra.

Dravite

The Stone of Hard Work

- The least known stone in the Tourmaline family
- Derived from Southeast Austria.
- High temperature and high-pressure mineral.

Metaphysical Healing Properties:

- It has a reassuring, relaxing and soothing effect on your body, your mind, and your heart.
- This stone will help you to descend from the higher planes and strongly connect with the earth.
- A cleansing stone that removes the negative energies and gives you more endurance when difficult situations arise.
- Helps teach you how to accept yourself.

- Will balance your mind and stimulate your imagination and creativity. It will enhance your experiences so that you have a fuller and more enlightening life.
- Will show you how you can accept yourself more deeply, especially the parts you have not accepted.

Physical Healing Properties:

- Known to assist the absorption of food nutrients. It can also correct bowel problems, especially the disease of Crohn's and irritable bowel syndrome.
- Can enhance the immune system and help the lymph system. It can heal the blood, reduce skin spots and treat other skin disorders.
- Dravite energies can help with sexual dysfunction.
- Very beneficial for loss of brain function, paralysis of the brain and autism. It is also known that it helps with ADD and ADHD.

Chakra: Solar Plexus Chakra, Sacral Chakra.

Serpentine

Stone of Elements

- Often mistaken for jade, similar in color and texture.
- Found in Russia, Switzerland, USA, and Canada.
- Stimulates the arousal od the kundalini energies.

Metaphysical Healing Properties:

- Works for clearing blocked or stagnant energy in any chakra.

- Perfect stone to help heal your heart from changes in relationships, be it a friend, a lover, or someone with whom you have a relationship.
- Relaxation of the emotional body, letting you surrender your fear of hardship and change so you can look ahead to the future with excitement and expectation.
- Will help you to be more willing to contribute to the greater good time and energy and less self-centered.
- Help you to not be too sensitive to other people's opinions, comments, or thoughts.

Physical Healing Properties:

- Supports efforts and rebalancing with digestion.
- Good for cleansing detoxifies the blood and the body.
- Treats hypoglycemia and diabetes.
- Isolates the aura, protecting delicate DNA and cell energy structures.
- Relieves Alzheimer's and senile dementia symptoms, relieves pain from bites, and stings. It corrects low blood sugar, diabetes, and weakness of your muscles.
- Inflammation of the skin, eczema, varicose veins, warts, skin, and parasites of the hair.

Chakra: Root Chakra, Crown Chakra.

Angelite

Stone of Peace

- Is said to be able to aid you in connecting with the angels and spirit world.
- Has soothing energy that is overall calming and helps you feel more peaceful.

- This stone was discovered most recently among all of the other stones.
- Originally discovered and mined in Peru.

Metaphysical Healing Properties:

- Useful for people who find it difficult to cope with incarnation, death, and sorrow.
- Stabilizes your feelings. and emotional and physical bodies.
- Calms and enhances creativity and psychic ability.
- Helps you to become more compassionate and accepting.
- Transmutes pain and disorder into wholeness and healing and opens the way to inspiration.
- creates a deep sense of tranquility and peace.

Physical Healing Properties:

- Treats throat disorders, especially those caused by difficulty expressing yourself.
- Removes the spinal fluid that has been retained and accumulated as well as disperses swelling.
- Balances the Thyroid and parathyroid systems.
- Used in weight control and relates to lungs and arms, in particular.
- Reparation of the tissue and blood vessels, balancing the fluids in the body.

Chakra: Crown Chakra, Heart Chakra.

Selenite
The Master

- One of the only healing crystals that do not have to be recharged at all, but can be used to clean and recharge any other crystals.
- Translucent and colorless.
- There are such large quantities of Quartz crystal, which are found in evaporated ancient seas and lakes. It is considered the most abundant of them all. Often found in Mexico and Brazil)
- Named after the Greek goddess of the moon, Selene.

Metaphysical Healing Properties:

- The utmost level of consciousness and everything that is infinite— intuition, the universe, and spirit guides.
- Excellent for meditation work, because it brings profound peace so that meditation or visualization can be more easily achieved.
- Related to spiritual activation and reaching higher planes.
- Through radiating light energy, it promotes purity and honesty.
- Brings clarity of the mind and opens the crown chakra.

Physical Healing Properties:

- Selenite can be used for almost anything. Taking the stone with you and meditating can contribute to inner peace and great healing.
- Aligns the spinal column and encourages flexibility, which helps to prevent epileptic seizures.

Chakra: Crown Chakra.

Pearlite

The Stone of Wonder

- Forms in other rock types.

- Petalite energizes and activates all of the body's energy centers when carried on the body.
- Has a high content of lithium.
- Emits energy and dissipates electromagnetic energy when placed in a room.

Metaphysical Healing Properties:

- Excellent for healing all types of emotional trauma, but especially valuable for overcoming the patterns of abuse and abuse victims.
- Provides calmness, self-acceptance, and self-love frequency.
- Can be used to soothe and balance traumatized emotions and energies
- Helps balance emotions by keeping mood swings at bay, let this stone remind you to invite and invoke angel's help to feel safe and safe.

Physical Healing Properties:

- Can be used for ADD, ADHD, excessive stress or worry.
- Helpful to regulate blood pressure and counter attacks on anxiety.
- Aids in endocrine system healing. It is useful for AIDS and cancer treatment. Cells, eyes, lungs, muscle spasms and intestines benefit.
- Supports you when the chemicals are out of whack in your brain and you are going through a manic period.

Chakra: Throat Chakra, Crown Chakra.

Heulandite

Stone of Emotion

- A type of Zeolite mineral.

- A wide range of colors.
- Considered a high vibration stone, and powerful for meditation.
- Is of a karmic nature.

Metaphysical Healing Properties:

- Excellent emotional healer for loss and grief.
- Controls sarcasm and criticism when needed.
- For connecting experiences of a past life that are relevant to you today.
- Helps to bring practical, focused and balanced change to your life to make you feel more wholesome. Powerful to help you make significant changes in your life.
- Creates beautiful vibration that opens mind, heart, and soul together and creates extraordinary spiritual activation.
- Enhances your psychic abilities, your spiritual vision, and your dreaming skills.

Physical Healing Properties:

- Can assist in weight loss, digestion processes, and the respiratory system.
- Improves mobility by improving movement and reducing pain in the joints.
- Repairs damage to the nervous system and liver.
- Encourages the efficient processing of nutrients and assists in overcoming food intolerances
- Eases breathing difficulties
- Unpacks complex illnesses into their component parts so that lingering viral or bacterial infection can be efficiently and effectively treated.

Chakra: Third-eye Chakra, Solar Plexus Chakra.

Amethyst

The Materialization Stone

- Along with Crystal Quartz and Selenite, Amethyst is one of the New Age's most famous stones.
- Amethyst can be found almost worldwide.
- Known for many things, this amazing purple crystal is more acknowledged for is the manifestation.

Metaphysical Healing Properties:

- Wonderful stone in a time of confusion or chaos.
- Amethyst allows you to connect your yearnings and purposes of life with your heart, and then you can materialize them into your life!
- Supports neural signal transmission through the brain.
- This powerful stone is linked to the upper chakras, which helps us bring the ethereal realm to the physical level. This includes the realization of our earthly dreams. Low, calming frequencies resonate.

Physical Healing Properties:

- Amethyst can relieve headaches, help boost the nervous system, balance hormones, treat insomnia, and alleviate neck tension. Place the crystal under the pillow in front of the bed to sleep soundly and wake refreshed, ready to manifest.
- Aids to the pituitary and pineal glands and can relieve hawthorns.
- Relieves physical, psychological and emotional pain or stress, and blocks geopathic stress.
- Encourages water reabsorption and insomnia treatment, bringing a restful sleep.

Chakra: Third eye Chakra, Crown Chakra.

Staurolite

Stone of Growth

- Quite unique, they naturally form a cross within the stone.
- Useful to help stop smoking
- Comes from the Greek word "Stauros" meaning 'cross'

Metaphysical Healing Properties:

- Stone of consolation for someone suffering from an illness or loss
- Reduces stress in the human body and helps you to gain respect by keeping to your views
- Give strength and patience to all those who carry the burdens of others
- Helps you feel safe, protected and secure
- Beneficial to emotions and can help counter hysteria, excessive fear, and paralysis of the emotions. Staurolite is useful for stress relief.

Physical Healing Properties:

- Strengthen muscles and help them grow.
- Staurolite brings alignment of body, mind, and spirit in order to achieve total health.
- Assists in building muscle and blood. This stone maintains your general physical health.
- Excellent to be used to counteract normal aging effects.
- Regenerates the body aftercare, care or recovery from bad habits and abuse of oneself.
- Treats cellular disorders and growth that increases carbohydrate assimilation and has traditionally been used for fever.

Chakra: Base Chakra, Third Eye Chakra, Crown Chakra.

Scapolite
Stone of Smarts

- Scapolite has been mined in Sri Lanka and Myanmar.
- Helpful stone for those of you who work at computers, this stone absorbs and disperses electromagnetic emissions from electrical equipment
- Stimulates psychic abilities

Metaphysical Healing Properties:

- Will help you understand how you may be using your power to manipulate other people's emotions or actions.
- Enables you to break self-destructive patterns, it is a stone for natal depression and PMS.
- Soothes the body in times of stress by releasing tension in the back, shoulders, and back.
- An extremely calming stone that will cut through confusion, distress, anger, and fear of going deep within your emotional center.
- Removes emotional garbage that is preventing you from moving forward
- Releases blocked energy from the body, especially in the legs and veins.

Physical Healing Properties:

- Said to unblock varicose veins, cataracts, and glaucoma also assists with bone disorders and the shoulders.
- Can be used to balance hyperactivity and inattentiveness.
- Enhances the healing of infection in the glands and glandular fever.

- Assists arthritis and bone problems and may help relieve the effects of Alzheimer's disease and dementia.

Chakra: Throat Chakra, Third-eye Chakra.

Moonstone
The Stabilizer

- Moonstone is closely connected to the feminine energy of the moon.
- Perfect for the graceful creation of harmony within one's intuition and for the strengthening of it.
- In ancient India, it was considered the stone of goddesses and gods and perfectly fit for the king.

Metaphysical Healing Properties:

- Increases patience and helps to remain objective when empathic information is received from others.
- Moonstones can open you to other worlds as well as to the universe.
- Can also be used to fight materialism and manage the ego by using the powerful tool of self-observation for self-improvement and spiritual growth.
- Improves emotional stability and control so that users can learn not to react to inappropriate situations that can lead to strong emotions.

Physical Healing Properties:

- Easily helps with eyes, hair, skin, and fleshy organs like the pancreas and the liver degenerative conditions.
- It can be used to aid with obesity, hormonal and menstrual problems, pituitary gland, retention of water, digestive system.

- helps insomnia
- Balances hormonal cycles and relieves period pain, cramps, pregnancy-related tensions, and a variety of other women's conditions.

Chakra: Third-eye Chakra, Solar Plexus Chakra.

Diopside
The Stone of Worry

- Called cats eye for its various stones in the shades of green
- A 4 rayed star
- Because of its crystal shape, named after a Greek word that translates into "double appearance."

Metaphysical Healing Properties:

- Will help you to reconcile with anyone or anything that has hurt you in the past by pushing you gently to take the first step.
- Promotes and enhances your ability to feel and honor your real feelings, feelings, and thoughts. Love, dedication, and inner heart.
- Beneficial to those who can not show sorrow because it shows that there is nothing wrong with your feelings and letting go.
- Increases the sense of compassion by opening your heart to other people's suffering.

Physical Healing Properties:

- Increases surgery recovery, trauma or serious disease.
- Stone supports the balance of cellular memory, physical weakness, acid and alkaline as well as hormones.

- Beneficial for heart and kidney inflammation, muscle aches, spasms, stress.
- Increases the circulatory system's heating and helps to eliminate toxins from the body.
- Can reduce fevers, aches, and pain in your body.

Chakra: Heart Chakra.

Kyanite

The Stone of Affliction

- Kyanite aids one's mind to make energy passageways where there used to be none, specifically with regard to meditation and emotional development.
- It doesn't collect energy so that the stone doesn't have to be cleaned and can be used to clean other stones and spaces.
- Chakras and subtle bodies that clear paths and meridians are instantly aligned.
- The soothing blue-green tone is reminiscent of the sky, making it particularly supportive and soothing for the nerves.

Metaphysical Healing Properties:

- It can also aid the ones who are transitioning through loss or death, mentally.
- As it takes meditation to a more significant depth, while opening channels to the spiritual realm, Kyanite may intensify psychic abilities.
- Lightens the burdens of emotion.
- Encourage you by cutting through fears and blockages to speak your truth.
- Opens the throat chakra and promotes communication and self-expression.
- Can help arbitration, in diplomatic missions, negotiations, and other forms of disharmonious communication.

- Helps spiritual energy manifest into thought processes, so that they can then manifest into reality.

Physical Healing Properties:

- It can be used to relieve headaches, tension around or on the brow, and pain in the eyes if you look too long at the computer.
- It can improve the ability to communicate and is great to help cure any throat pain.
- Resolves respiratory health issues.
- Natural reliever of pain reduces blood pressure and cures infections.
- Can help bridge the energy gaps because of surgery and other intrusive trauma that aids tissues and nerves restore tracts throughout the trauma site, just like bone breakage.

Chakra: Throat Chakra, Brow Chakra, Heart Chakra.

Cinnabar

The Stone of Alignment

- Known as dragon's blood.
- Is toxic due to its mercury content, but is safe to wear.

Metaphysical Healing Properties:

- Connects with the acceptance that everything is in place at this moment and as it should be.
- Releases energy blocks and aligns energy centers
- Promotes longevity, physical warming, elevated mood, anti-suicide, and anti-senility.
- Focuses your life in the physical world rather than the spiritual world.
- Will make you more aware of the passing of time and your life moving along.

Physical Healing Properties:

- Excellent for treating deep-seated or systematic wounds, whether viral or bacterial
- Helps stimulate the immune system and purify the blood. It can be helpful in treating HIV, herpes, staph and strep infections.
- Useful in warts, lesions, and boils healing.
- Can be used to balance issues of sexual energy and fertility. Increases sales and cash flow in a business environment or work environment.

Chakra: Sacral Chakra, Root Chakra.

Aventurine

The Stone of Opportunity

- Well known for enhancing good luck, prosperity and wealth.
- A variety of quartz that attracts luck and helps new opportunities to be successfully exploited.

Metaphysical Healing Properties:

- In association with the heart chakra, Aventurine also generates a sense of emotional calm and general well-being, which also helps anxiety.
- Aventurine harmonizes emotional, physical and mental bodies and restores balance. Promotes wellness, compassion, and empathy and embraces perseverance.
- Encourages emotional recovery and enables your own heart to wish to live.

Physical Healing Properties:

- This stone supports the circulation of the heart, blood, and energy.
- Benefits the thymus gland, the tissue, and the nervous system.
- gives the body an anti-inflammatory effect.
- Works to heal the adrenals, lungs, sinuses, heart and muscle system.
- Can also help to accelerate recovery from injury, disease or surgery.

Chakra: Third eye Chakra, Throat Chakra, Solar Plexus Chakra, Sacral Chakra, and Heart Chakra.

Bronzite

Stone of Harmony

- Provides a dynamic state of nonaction and nondoing.
- Promotes positivity and is called Bronzite because of its resemblance to the element Bronze.
- Used mainly for protection purposes.

Metaphysical Healing Properties:

- Bronzite is effective against curses, a magical protector and turns negative thoughts and bad desires right back.
- Helps us with certainty and with our actions.
- Supports self-affirmation, restores composure and keeps the head cool.
- Helpful for stress overcoming and voluntary revision.

Physical Healing Properties:

- Support and balance the psyche's body with yin and yang energy.

- Aided for chronic exhaustion, iron assimilation, cramps, and nerves.
- Used in crystal healing for solar plexus chakra-related ailments.
- Assists in the reduction of muscle tension and the dissipation of agitation caused by emotional and psycho-physical disorders.

Chakra: Solar Plexus Chakra, Root Chakra.

Biotite
The Gold Stone

- Sometimes called "black mica"
- Can only be found in Canada, Sicily, and Russia.
- Named after the fresh physicist, who studied and investigated the optical properties of the stone.
- Often mistaken for gold

Metaphysical Healing Properties:

- Provides us with reflective qualities so that we can recognize our civilization's shortcomings while keeping our heart centered so that we can love what we see here.
- Helps us to get rid of anger, tantrums and nervous energy.
- Balances your ambitions with all your sense of compassion and fosters more kindness and understanding of the people with whom you interact with every day.
- Supports information maintenance and order within the mind.
- Promotes clarity and balances too much psychological perception and reduces your overwhelming psychological impressions.

- Helps release energy blocks and align chakras inside the body.

Physical Healing Properties:

- Used to diagnose diseases and disorders associated with disorganized cellular patterns.
- Used to treat eye problems, throat and voice conditions as well.
- Can help increase the energy flow at specific body locations.
- It helps to improve and maintain tissue, cell, and bone marrow health.
- A good stone to boost brain function and improve the functions of the neurological system as a whole.

Chakra: Heart Chakra, Crown Chakra.

Obsidian

The Mirror Stone

- This stone is the result from volcanic lava coming in contact with water, this process is what gives the black rock a gloss-like texture that looks like glass.
- It's a highly reflective surface and consistent coloring enables you to look deep inside to divulge your soul and the necessary healing to increase your vibration.
- This jet black stone is known as the mirror stone for its sight-enhancing power, the way you see the world and the circumstances of it.

Metaphysical Healing Properties:

- Obsidian dates back to the Stone Age, it is known to allow views of realms accessible from earth, of the soul itself, and of other worlds.

- Used to gain knowledge and wisdom.
- Use this to unravel your own flaws, weaknesses, and shadow so that you can understand yourself furthermore.
- Helps you identify outdated behavioral patterns and helps clean them.

- Shock and fear dissolve with it.
- Use obsidian to alleviate wiped out memory, ignored, or even long buried emotional distress.
- It can be utilized to relieve emotional trauma anxiety and stress.
- Helps you cope with sorrow, loss and separation pain.

Physical Healing Properties:

- Aids in digestion and detoxification, blockage and tension dissolving, including hardened arteries.
- If you have been shocked by injury, it will be dissolved on a cellular level and therefore helps staunch bleeding and accelerates wound healing.
- Reduces arthritis pain, joint pain, cramps, and injuries.
- Helps improve blood flow circulation.

Chakra: Base Chakra.

Seraphinite

The Stone of Serendipity

- This crystal can be found only in Sabena Lake Baikal, Russia.
- The name derives from its perceived link with seraphim, the highest order of angels due to the inclusion of feather-like mica in the stone.

Metaphysical Healing Properties:

- Every emotion is said to be removed.
- Helps to release emotional energies that don't serve. It brings the emotional body enlightenment and joyful energy and stimulates the flow and elasticity of your energy, ensuring you can react emotionally in a balanced and harmonious way.
- Cleanse feelings that do not serve you anymore by bringing clarity to the source of emotional imbalances.

Physical Healing Properties:

- Helps to release the belief systems or patterns that lead to the manifestation of the same physical diseases or diseases that you or your family members suffer.
- You can choose a different outcome with this stone and focus on breaking the pattern.
- Assists in regulating the growth and reproduction of all cancer cell types.
- Blood strengthener and can assist in cellular respiration and the delivery of nutrients to the cells.

Chakra: Heart Chakra, Crown Chakra.

Crystal Quartz

The Spirit Stone

- Crystal quartz in the metaphysical world is regarded as the most famous light window.
- A wide range of rock varieties can be found and is extremely abundant. • Supports your overall wellness essentially.
- This stone's clarity and understanding often alleviate disturbing feelings.

Metaphysical Healing Properties:

- This particular crystal contains the whole color spectrum and can be used from the spirit world to the physical world to amplify desires, prayers, and manifestations.
- Meditate the crystal with your intentions with this stone, and "program." This particular crystal contains the whole color range and can be used to increase desires, prayers, and manifestations from the spirit world to the physical world.
- Helps you stay focused on the objective at hand. The stone is useful for recalling memory, so use it for examinations or testing.
- Increase your ability to succeed in all life-related activities, including fertility, financial security, family, creativity, a happy home, a healthy body, blessings and more.

Physical Healing Properties:

- A master healing stone designed to stimulate the immune and circulatory systems, and also to increase the chi energy flow in the body.
- Stimulates the nervous system and fingernail and hair growth
- Can help remove bonding tissue adhesions.

Chakra: Crown Chakra.

Blue Topaz

The Stone of Creativity

- The bright blue color of this stone reflects the mind to learn more quickly and retain information that almost the rest of your life can draw on.
- It also helps to fire creativity and to open the mind to fresh ideas.

Metaphysical Healing Properties:

- Topaz is a mental stone, great to connect with one's spirit guides, loved ones who have passed on, and angels.
- Use topaz to open your soul, align with the realm of spirit, and expand your mind.
- Calms strong emotions and helps clear the mind with a sense of peace and tranquility.
- Inspires leadership and supports clear communication and natural authority.
- Helps you let go of anger and resentment, makes it easier for you and others to surrender to forgiveness.
- Help you control anger feelings by bringing hidden emotions calmly to the surface so that they can be treated in a positive way.

Physical Healing Properties:

- Ideal for treating liver and digestive system problems.
- It has always been known to help with eye disease, mental illness, dimness in sight, and to restore taste loss.
- Improve throat healing, eyes, ears, and nasal passage disease.
- The metabolism increases and the thyroid energizes.
- Reduces menopause side effects.
- Regenerates and revitalizes the physical body. It delays the aging process, disperses negative energy that attempts to weaken your resistance to disease.

Chakra: Sacral Chakra, Solar Plexus Chakra.

Hematite

The Grounding Stone

- This iron-rich stone is deeply grounded and earth-related.
- In ancient Greece, it was referred to as the " bloodstone" because of the red hue of the iron content found in nature.

Metaphysical Healing Properties:

- Hematite is linked to the root chakra and has a deeply grounded energy that reminds us of our human existence.
- Perfect stone to keep you out of " drama. "
- Excellent to organize your thoughts. Balances self-esteem and self-vision by the negative.
- Can be used to relieve anxiety about stress and to calm the nervous system.
- Supports financial stability flow.

Physical Healing Properties:

- Iron found in hematite can help us clean the blood, improve circulation, manage irregular menstrual flow and promote healthy heart conditions.
- Due to its grounding properties, it can relieve symptoms exacerbated by stress or anxiety.
- Positive heart and circulatory system effects.

Chakra: Root Chakra.

Citrine

The Money Stone

- Type of quartz with a golden yellow hue, the yellow colors of money, gold and wealth are associated.
- Powerful cleanser and regenerator that carry the sun's power are warming, energizing, and highly creative.
- Never require cleaning.
- Can guide you significantly in meditation when you make the most of your unique talents, you can easily enter a peaceful, calm meditative state using this stone.

Metaphysical Healing Properties:

- Take this stone to the bank, to financial business meetings, or place it on your desk while you are working.
- helps to understand information, analyze and guide situations in a positive direction. Makes you less critical, helps you develop a positive attitude and flow rather than in the past.
- Encourages inner calm to enable wisdom to emerge. Citrine can help you gain wealth, financial wealth and stability.
- Increases self-esteem in order to reduce self-injurious behaviors.

Physical Healing Properties:

- Citrine stimulates metabolism, helps to digest other conditions affecting the gastrointestinal system and nausea.
- Can also be used to boost nerve impulses, helping the brain to fire quickly and sharply.
- Facilitates the cure of ache, bedwetting, depression, diabetes, birth, sadness and problems of growth.
- Supports your mental and energy efforts.
- Purifies chakras.

Chakra: Crown Chakra, Solar Plexus Chakra, and Sacral Chakra.

Pearl

Gemstone of the Sea

- In contrast to other earth gemstones, pearls are formed in fresh and saltwater mollusks.
- If used, will make you wiser.

Metaphysical Healing Properties:

- A stone that will cultivate your inner wisdom, it will also show you how in your life to strengthen and nurture love.

Physical Healing Properties:

- Provides crystal healing by helping to treat disorders of the digestive tract and muscular system.
- It also helps maintain or restore your body's balance and natural rhythm. It can also regulate your hormone level.
- Beneficial for lung patients, such as chronic bronchitis, asthma, and tuberculosis;
- Helps with healing the heart and liver, urinary system, kidneys.

Chakra: Sacral Chakra.

Jade
The Dream Stone

- Another dynamic stone to be found throughout the world in a multitude of colors.
- Region ordinarily dictates stone color.
- Jade in ancient times was one of the most commonly used stones.

Metaphysical Healing Properties:

- The stone represents the ranking nobility and ideals.
- Promote autonomy and independence in an engaged relationship. If you are deeply attracted to this attraction of a stone, you may have an existential crisis and seek some reassurance.
- Jade promotes happiness and harmony in family life and in romantic relationships with you.
- This stone is connected to the heart and helps us to accept the truth, to express love (to oneself and to others) and to reach shamanic realms in the dream state.

Physical Healing Properties:

- Jade is good for filtering toxins and cleaning the body as a whole through the bloodstream in combination with the heart.
- A stone that can heal and soothe both the nervous system and the kidneys, gallbladder and the liver. It can help the renal system to remove kidney stones. Promotes cell recovery.
- Can reduce pain related to cramps, joints, and aches of the bone.
- Can also be used after surgery to relieve joint pain and accelerate the healing process.

Chakra: Third-eye Chakra, Sacral Chakra.

Opal

The Eye Stone

- When moved into the light, this brilliant and colorful stone appears to be on fire with a rainbow spectrum of electric colors.
- It is related to the eye, as it is so pleasant to look, and to the Third Eye Chakra.
- A popular belief in France was that Opal could make his or her wearer invisible so that he or she could steal without being caught.
- There are more than 10 different opal types, all from different parts of the world with slightly different characteristics.

Metaphysical Healing Properties:

- Opal acts as a prism of the whole aura and brings the spiritual and energy body into the whole spectrum of light.
- Vibrant energy that is not commonly seen from other stones can be amplified in the soul.
- stimulates originality and dynamic creativity, helps you to access your true self and express it. Reinforces desire, eroticism, and sexuality. It makes us emotional, seductive, and unconventional and makes you love your life.
- Opal inspires optimism, happiness, appreciation, and welfare.
- Use Opal to awaken psychological and mystical qualities and connect ancient spiritual realms as a vehicle.

Physical Healing Properties:

- The Opal, referred to as the eye stone, can be used to promote eye health and improve vision.
- Treat the disease, infection, and fever of Parkinson.
- Memory can also be stimulated and neurotransmitter disturbances stabilized.
- Reinforces the will to live.
- Opal is beneficial to eye, kidney and skin health.
- Helpful if you are in need of dehydration or retention of water.

Chakra: All because of the variety of colors.

Fuchsite

Stone of Collecting

- Translucent to transparent crystals.
- Can be found almost anywhere.
- Fuchsite is really good for the function of blood cells and the body.
- Comes in colors of all types

Metaphysical Healing Properties:

- Collects unwanted emotions to cleanse and release the heart chakra, calms the process.
- Fosters light-heartedness, friendliness, compassion, and recovery from exercises that are spiritually damaging.
- Helps you understand your interactions with others and links to life's fundamental concerns.
- Releases you through sacrificial service to others from creating or maintaining your identity and self-value.

Physical Healing Properties:

- Helps to reduce swelling and pain caused by carpel tunnel syndrome.
- Aid for spinal alignment, muscles, immune system, throat, inflammation and sleep disorders.
- Helps relieve nausea
- More coordinated domestic schedules, such as childcare, school runs, visits to elderly or sick relationships and work commitments, can be provided when placed in your home.

Chakra: Heart Chakra.

Peacock Ore

Stone of Happiness

- Mainly used for decorative or cosmetic purposes.
- When exposed to some air, the colors change, making it look like a peacock with all the colors.
- is known for the effect of happiness it gives.

Metaphysical Healing Properties:

- This stone promotes awareness of inner wealth and awareness that wealth only comes from within.
- Helps us to cope with stress and obstacles blocking our path to a specific objective.
- helps to identify new ways and opportunities that can help us achieve our dreams and objectives.
- Helpful stone to protect against negative energy, it can also help you to recognize negative energy more clearly.
- Can stimulate your inner spirit to reach further heights, thus enhancing your ability to enjoy the momentary happiness.
- Useful to re-birth and to bring your emotions together with your intellect.

Physical Healing Properties:

- Synchronizes the cellular structure and metabolism of our body.
- Supports fever reduction and swelling.
- It helps to regulate adrenaline flow in our bodies.
- Blood circulation is also known to increase if you place it under the waist.
- Maintains the body's electrolyte balance.

Chakra: has the ability to align all of the Chakras.

Agate
Stone of Inner Stability

- You can find this varied stone in almost all colors with seemingly endless striation types.
- Often found as layers lining Geodes ' internality.
- Strong chakras relationships.
- Agate incarnates the inner world and all its states.

Metaphysical Healing Properties:

- Agate raises self-consciousness, stabilizes the aura (in all its colors), transforms negative energy and is a powerful spiritual conduit.
- Agate gives you protection, security, and security by dissolving internal tensions, enabling you to withstand eternal influences better.
- Has the power to harmonize your yin and yang with the positive and negative forces in place in the universe. Gently facilitates self-acceptance, builds self-confidence.
- Use the stone to cure anger, emotional instability and feelings of self-worthlessness.

Physical Healing Properties:

- Known to enhance mental function by improving thought clarity.
- Good for centering assistance and physical energy establishment.
- Heals the eyes, stomach, uterus and cleanses the pancreas and lymphatic system.
- Agate is a wonderful stone to use when writing or gathering thoughts for a meaningful conversation with someone you care about and want to communicate clearly with before an important test.
- Useful for reprogramming cellular memory in a previous or present life after mortification of the flesh, emotions or spirit.
- Aids in hidden circumstances self-analysis and perception, bringing to your attention any disease that interferes with your well-being.

Chakra: Crown Chakra.

Moldavite

Rock of Glass

- Most often found in deserts.
- A transparent green type of glass that is thought to be formed by an impact on the surface of the earth by a meteor or other extraterrestrial object that causes the soil to cool and recrystallize into a tektite.
- It has been used as a talisman since the stone age.

Metaphysical Healing Properties:

- Moldovite brings you into contact with the higher self and improves other crystals.
- It takes you into the highest spiritual dimension and facilitates the process of ascension. Before using the stone, you must be grounded or you can feel spacious and rootless.
- Eliminates the blockages and aligns the chakras.
- The divine integrates and speeds up spiritual growth.
- Opens the chakra of the crown to receive the highest spiritual direction.
- Assists in developing worldly separation, worries about money and the future. It emphasizes qualities like empathy and compassion.

Physical Healing Properties:

- A great diagnostic tool that highlights the disease source and also supports the healing process due to its high vibrational energy.
- Prevents mental degeneration, retention of memory, balance maintenance and more.
- Infections of the respiratory tract, allergies, gout, and anemia also help.

Chakra: Crown Chakra.

Jet

Stone of Age

- A fossilized wood coalition that comes from a family of tall evergreen cone-bearing trees in South America and Australia.
- Been long used as a talisman.
- Usually black or brown.
- Could be significantly amplified if paired with other stones.

Metaphysical Healing Properties:

- Jet can be used to open yourself to psychic experiences and help you on your path to spiritual illumination.
- Balances mood swings, relieves depression and brings balance and stability.
- Works with you to restore your lost balance and harmony.
- Can attract knowledge and wisdom to deepen the meaning of your life.
- Will add excitation and fulfillment so that you can always look forward to something.

Physical Healing Properties:

- A migraine, epilepsy, bowel problems, mouth problems, grinding of teeth, gum disease and colds.
- Can decrease glandular and lymph swelling and cure pain in the stomach.
- Can cure aches of the stomach and menstrual cramps.
- Addresses health issues related to stress or sadness.
- Can also be used with people suffering from epilepsy.

Chakra: Root chakra.

Amazonite

The Stone of Courage

- Amazonite claims the spirit and soothes the greenish color of the soul.
- This stone enables you, without being overly emotional, to seek and express your inner truth with courage and conviction.
- Electromagnetic pollution protection.

Metaphysical Healing Properties:

- Used for balancing and cleaning all chakras.
- Helps you gain insight into a problem on both sides and helps to dispel aggravating and negative energy.
- Amazonite can relieve emotional trauma stored in the body and help prevent this trauma from manifesting into a physical disease.
- It is also useful to harmonize the relationship between intellect and intuition for a sound and well-founded balance.

Physical Healing Properties:

- Amazonite is typically used for well-being and is beneficial to the whole body.
- Calms the brain and nervous system and aligns the physical body with ethereal health.
- When used properly, negative energy dissipates and helps the nervous system.
- Use it, in particular, to soothe rashes, clear acne and prevent wound infection.
- Supports the absorption of calcium via parathyroid and thyroid.

Chakra: Heart Chakra, Throat Chakra.

Onyx

Stone of Sadness

- Onyx crystal name is derived from the Latin and Greek languages. It means " claw" or " fingernail."
- It consists of fine silica mineral growths.

Metaphysical Healing Properties:

- Heals grief that has lasted too long and helps to repair the heart.
- Assist in providing mental focus, grounding, and the ability to remain on the job.
- Gives support in mental or physical stressful times and in confusing or difficult situations.
- Stimulates the basic chakra and helps you to ground and connect to the Earth's electromagnetic energy.
- Onyx helps you learn lessons by giving you self-confidence and helping you feel comfortable in your environment.
- Can enhance spiritual vision and dream experiences related to that.

Physical Healing Properties:

- Enhances your financial strength and your ability to remain focused and achieve financial objectives.
- Can help to decrease the symptoms of headaches and to strengthen the eyes and optical nerves;
- Benefits for teeth, bone marrow, disorders of blood and feet.
- Increases general stamina and self-control.

Chakra: Root Chakra.

Tourmaline

The Grounding Stone

- Preferred protective talisman, tourmaline is used as a psychic shield to base your energy on the entry into your energy field of negative entities.
- Long used by magicians, shamans, witches, and wizards.
- Tourmaline can be found on all continents.

Metaphysical Healing Properties:

- As a black stone that acts as a sponge for harmful or dark energies, it absorbs light. It encourages you to stay shining in dark times.
- It is utilized to elevate your vibration and bring you into the light, keep away negative energies, even if it is black as night.
- Balances the right and left brain hemispheres and turns negative energies into positive ones.
- Removes obsessive or compulsive behaviors and releases chronic anxiety and anxiety.
- Attracts inspiration, compassion, tolerance, and prosperity.

Physical Healing Properties:

- Use tourmaline to relieve joint pain and help re-align the spine.
- It can also be used to strengthen the immune system, heart and adrenal glands–stress relief and tension release. Benefits the brain and the pulmonary. It corrects fluid disequilibrium by treating the kidneys, bladder, thymus, and thyroid.
- Insomnia, night sweats, sinusitis, and bacterial infections are helpful. Eases neck disease, pituitary disease, adrenal disease, and all major glands.

Chakra: Base Chakra, Throat, and Heart Chakra.

Phenacite

The Rare Stone

- Crystallizes often in short, hexagonal prisms.
- Advanced crystal workers are recommended.
- Comes from the Greek word meaning ' deceiver. ' This is because other crystals are easily mistaken for how varied they are in formations.
- Stone searched for due to its high energy, frequency, and vibration.

Metaphysical Healing Properties:

- Can relieve feelings of desperation and fear of change and make you more aware of the benefits of becoming a group or a community's energies.
- Phenacite helps increase your resolve so that your life can be changed to reflect more of your emotional and spiritual purpose.
- Allows you to access higher levels of consciousness and guidance quickly. It activates the third eye, the crown and the etheric chakras above the head, fostering mental perception, vision, and dreams of power.
- Can deepen meditation and help to bring into reality the high self-consciousness.
- Stimulates the light body by clear and pure light.

Physical Healing Properties:

- Excellent for nerve damage, brain imbalances, brain damage and genetic disorders that limit the function of the brain.
- Ease nausea and pain caused by migraine and headaches.

- Helps diseases in which conventional medicine does not work or in which chemotherapy, radiotherapy, genetic disorder or AIDS / HIV have weakened the body.
- Assists in stimulating and enhancing different aspects of brain function and brain activity.

Chakras: Third-Eye chakra.

Quantum Quattro

Stone of Transformations.

- Found in Namibia.
- Works at higher vibrational energy than other stones.

Metaphysical Healing Properties:

- Will inspire you through kindness and gentleness to express your own personal power.
- Supports tough love, but also shows where intervention would have a positive outcome and teaches you to walk away from everything that will not help your growth.
- Dissolves negative emotions such as solar plexus chakra guilt and grief, reverses destructive emotional programming and cures injury, betrayal, sorrow, and abandonment.
- Inspires creativity and environmental concert.
- This stone will help you to correct the imbalance whenever you feel something is off or out of alignment.
- Promotes a healthy, natural flow of energy and spiritual activation.
- The clearing of attachments, blockages, cords and karmic contracts can help.

Physical Healing Properties:

- Increases immune system healing, blood oxygenation, lungs, pancreas, addiction, thyroid, metabolism, and thymus.
- Increases the detoxification of all organs and systems, particularly intestines, liver, lungs, and kidney.
- Digestive, circulatory, reproductive and endocrine system healing.
- Can relieve arthritis pain, help with heart disease and control blood pressure.
- Can be useful for people who suffer from diabetes and calcium deficiencies.

***Chakra*:** Solar Plexus Chakra, Throat Chakra, the Heart chakra.

Garnet
The Stone of Health and Creativity

- This highly vibrating and grounded stone is found in a variety of colors and compositions almost everywhere in the world.
- Most known for his ability to promote health and creativity and bring spirit to earth.

Metaphysical Healing Properties:

- Garnet helps eliminate taboos and inhibitions.
- Revitalizes, purifies, and balances energy with the necessary serenity of passion at the time.
  • Inspires devotion and love.
- Allows the mind to think as freely and creatively as possible.
- Invites the spirit to participate in the physical realm and opens the channels of communication and creativity to external expression with the inner self.

- Has a connection to the hypnosis and can raise spiritual awareness of oneself.
- Boosts sexual expression and neutralizes the emotional aspect.

Physical Healing Properties:
- Garnet is a wonderful stone, known to stimulate the metabolism of the body, to make things flow in the body and, additionally, to help coagulate blood and stop bleeding.
- Works to restore the circulatory system through toxin cleaning and blood purification.
- Encourages blood formation and boosts the liver functions.
- It's also used to improve sexual libido and the heart's desires.

Chakra: Base Chakra, Heart Chakra.

Peridot
Stone of Evolution

- Assists in all kinds of transitions, especially that help you to rise above addiction.
- Egypt is where the best quality of this stone is found.

Metaphysical Healing Properties:
- This stone can help you to have the courage to fulfill your heart's wishes, to be generous to others, even as you pursue your own destiny.
- Protection against destructive jealousy caused by betrayal in past relationships and personal fears that you are unlovable, rather than in relation to the present relationship.

- Helps eliminate blockages to receive good energy, many spiritual people are adapted to give love, energy and time, but they may not be as good at receiving it.
- Makes you aware of the things that you have neglected to do and encourages you to compensate for the damage in healthy ways.
- Help you to think outside the box by opening your mind to the world's unlimited possibilities.

Physical Healing Properties:

- Strong detoxification effects and improves the overall functioning of the liver.
- Increases hepatic and gallbladder function stimulates metabolism and helps with skin problems, including warts.
- Will help to stimulate overdue work on the body, and to alleviate swelling and any unwanted growths.
- Can be used to mitigate heart heaviness and all kinds of heart-related imbalances.
- Helps to strengthen the blood circulation and to combat anemia and poor oxygenation in the lungs.

Chakra: Solar Plexus Chakra, Heart Chakra.

Rose Quartz

The Love Stone

- Pink shades of Quarts are associated with the heart and expressing unconditional love to self, others, and the planet.

Metaphysical Healing Properties:

- A magnificent stone to invite love, to help give love and even to attract your soul mate. Rose Quartz is heavily associated with the heart and heart chakra.

- It's a good stone for sorrow, loss of love, loss of friendship and better connection with children and babies.
- Impacts empathy, sensitivity and, at times, sensitivity on self-love, a strong stone for the heart, romance and allowing the ability to love wholeheartedly.
- To open yourself to finding love, carry or wear rose quartz. If you are in a relationship, it can help to deepen and nurture your love to each other.

Physical Healing Properties:

- Repairs and reinforces circulatory systems, releases body impurities, and helps with problems of the chest and lungs.
- When centered around the heart chakra, it is known to improve circulation and reduce blood pressure and can be used for deep emotional release and healing.
- Can also be used for reducing Virgo, easing palpitations or skipped beats and releasing tension.
- Cleans the body of toxins and excess fluids and makes it an ideal treatment crystal for water retention and edema conditions.

Chakra: Heart Chakra.

Ruby

Stone of Age

- Ancient legends in Myanmar say that you would become invincible by inserting a ruby into your flesh.
- Believed to communicate very good overall health to everybody that comes in contact with it.
- Lends you lifestyle and vigor.

Metaphysical Healing Properties:

- If you've lacked enthusiasm and feel generally bored, the ruby's energy will help to flow your blood.
- Intensifies your life passions and the emotions that are related to them.
- A talisman can be used to bring fortune, joy, sexual vigor, love, and power.
- Provides healthy tension and dynamism, enthusiastically motivates you and lifts you out of lethargy and exhaustion. It also has an impact on hyperactivity.

Physical Healing Properties:

- Can warm and energize even the most sluggish of auras, and as such is excellent for people who are convalesced or infirm.
- Can help cure infections, lower cholesterol, reduce blood clots, detoxify the blood and eliminate sobering difficulties.
- Stimulates circulation, menses and the pituitary gland, it is an excellent stone to keep your person cured of blood-related disorders or problems with blood pressure.
- It can often be used to treat sexual dysfunction and infertility to control your weight.
- Stimulates spleen, adrenal glands, and circulation as a whole.
- It helps to overcome infectious diseases like intestine diseases or flesh-eating bacteria's.

Chakras: Sacral Chakra, Third-eye Chakra, Heart Chakra.

Turquoise

The Stone of Safety

- Believed to be one of man's oldest known stones.

- Chiefs, shamans, kings, wizards and the like have long cherished Turquoise.
- In almost all ancient cultures, awarded as a symbol of wisdom, turquoise has been prevalent and has always been known as a protective stone.

Metaphysical Healing Properties:

- Shields emotion and heals irregular heartbeats and heartbreak.
- Turquoise strengthens the body's meridians and promotes intuition and better meditation.
- Connects physical and spiritual awareness, development and relaxation of inner strength.
- Helps you develop a sense of empathy for other people.
- Balances extreme mood fluctuation and dissolves an apathetic attitude of self-martyrdom. The brain is also refreshed if you are tired.
- It is also linked to the throat chakra, which supports clear communication with oneself and people around you, because of its blue hue.
- Turquoise is a talisman of protection and it channels the ancient wisdom it emits.

Physical Healing Properties:

- Assists with the brain, neck, ears, and throat issues.
- Assists with healing problems of the liver, anemia, health of the blood, nerve endings, physical strength, mobility, ear infections, and inner ear problems.
- Turquoise is strongly associated with the psychic realm, making it useful for clearing blockages and supporting the healthy flow of energy within the body, a truly great stone.
- Can help to improve vision, throat problems, bladder, weakness, the acidity of the stomach and issues in the stomach.

Chakra: Third Eye Chakra, Throat Chakra, Heart Chakra.

Diamond

The Stone of Colors

- Derived from the Greek word "Adamas" which means "invincible." This is precisely the theme that passes through the whole diamond mythology.
- Big symbol of courage and strength.
- For thousands of years, it was seen as a sign of wealth, and it still is today.
- The most popular gemstone in the world and most sought after.
- Was used to explore the spectrum of colors.
- Has been used as a purity symbol since ancient times.

Metaphysical Healing Properties:

- Their power productivity can be increased when used with other crystals.
- Clears mental and emotional pain, brings new beginnings to life, and reduces fear.
- Highly creative stone that stimulates your imagination and creative flow.
- Increase your personality, ethics, and fidelity to your own ideas and place in the world.
- helps you to overcome fear, depression and a sense of meaninglessness in life.
- Helps to promote harmony and balance in a partnership, marriage, or relationship.

Physical Healing Properties:

- Assists in the physical cure of concentration problems, artery sclerosis, bad memory, sight weakening, eye disease, gout, strokes, and cataracts.
- Strengthens blood vessels and glands that help blood flow.
- Heals organ diseases that directly affect mental functions in the brain.
- Ideal for people who have recently had a stroke, can initially reduce symptoms and helped you continue your life with little to no problems.

***Chakra*:** Third-eye Chakra, Solar Plexus Chakra.

Fluorite

The Stone of Positivity

- One of the most undervalued but also among one of the most powerful stones.
- Known to suck negative energy and low vibrations from a space or your body quite literally and create space for light to shine in.
- Fluorite is actually a magic crystal found in multiple color variations.

Metaphysical healing properties:

- Used to raise your vibration, alchemize negative energy and calm a chaotic mind, used for auric protection among most people.
- Makes you more aware of emotions that you have suppressed. It does not emphasize its expression, however, but helps you gradually bring it to the surface.
- Fosters impartiality and diseases relating to the eyes, mouth, and ears.
- Rainbow Fluorite is best known to stabilize your mind, amplify your psychic connection and enhance your intuitive abilities.

- Neutralizes excess emotional energy by encouraging a better flow of energy throughout the chakras.

Physical Healing Properties:

- This dynamic stone can be used to clear your mind and sharpen your focus when studying.
- Can help with osteoporosis by reinforcing your spine and promoting a more upright posture, helps with stiffness and joint problems.
- Can also be used to relieve body inflammation, to dissipate cold symptoms and to cure the mucous membrane. Impacts the body, strengthening it and making it more resistant to illness and injury.
- Assists with dizziness, vertigo or disruptive off balance issues.

Chakra: Third eye Chakra, Throat Chakra, Heart Chakra.

Amber

The Stone of Self

- Amber dates back to around 2000 B.C. Or before that.
- Actually composed of tree resin and sticky semi-liquid, which has been hardened over the years.
- Technically, Amber should be considered a fossil and not a crystal, but is very often used in pieces of jewelry that incorporate high-class gemstones.
- Sometimes they have insects and pieces of nature formed within them.
- Found in the ancient tombs of Egypt as well as incorporated onto the tops of the tombs.

Metaphysical Healing Properties:

- This golden resin is highly protective against negative events. Especially useful if the negative is from psychological sources.
- Warm and bright energies of Ambers are transferred to a sunny, spontaneous arrangement which respects tradition from which Amber was made famous.
- Could help to counter suicidal and thoughts of depression. Links the spiritual self to the physical every day reminding you why you are here.
- Balances and encourages patience when decision-making.
- Strong stone to contribute to generating creativity for any occasion.

Physical Healing Properties:

- Relieves heart problems, arthritis, and pain absorbing.
- Encourages the balance and healing of your digestive system, adrenals, stomach, liver, and gallbladder.
- Allows the body to work on healing itself and restoring overall balance.
- Amber is a powerful cleanser and healer that helps to cure body diseases and revitalizes tissue that has been affected in any way.
- Assists in nutrient assimilation throughout the body, especially nutrient deficiencies.

Chakra: Solar Plexus Chakra Root Chakra, Throat Chakra.

Carnelian

The Stone of Action

- Used to guide and protect the dead, often used in burials thousands of years ago.

- The color depends on the crystals iron level and how old it is.
- Can help to clear bad energy when placed with other stones.
- Keeps an improved flow of life energy running through the blood.

Metaphysical Healing Properties:

- Accelerates your motivation and helps you clarify your objectives so that you can find the best direction in your life and exactly what you want.
- Grounds you and actually anchors you when you are feeling sad emotions.
- Excellent for motivation and vitality restoration in the older.
- Carnelian can encourage initiative, boldness, assertiveness, dramatic abilities, and affability when used correctly.

Physical Healing Properties:

- Heals uterus, fallopian tubes, ovaries, cervixes, tubes, and pelvis reproductive systems.
- Influences the reproductive organs of both men and women by increasing fertility, overcoming impotence and frigidity.
- Helps with bad inflammatory arthritis, mostly in the hands.
- Increases your metabolism and contributes to back issues that may be bothering you.
- It can help to stop severe bleeding if carnelian is placed directly on the bleeding wound.

Chakra: Heart chakra Throat Chakra.

Sodalite

Stone of Balance

- Found in the United States, Canada, Italy, India, and Brazil.

- Most commonly known as an Ornamental gemstone.
- Named for connection to Sodium.

Metaphysical Healing Properties:

- Balances rampant emotions, very helpful for your anger and frustration, to calm and release.
- Helps you to recognize and accept that your emotional problems are usually based on fluctuating hormone, estrogen, progesterone and testosterone levels.
- Helps you deal with releasing negative emotions and expressing them in a less aggressive, harmful way.
- Can reduce stress and anxiety by enabling you to see your reality from a higher and calmer perspective.
- Dissolves feelings of guilt and enables you to stand up for yourself and live your own feelings whatever they may be.

Physical Healing Properties:

- Reduces the body's calming energy inflammation and also relieves inflammatory conditions such as headaches and muscle strain.
- Can be used to help control blood pressure and to facilitate retention of water. Has a cooling effect and stimulates bodily fluid absorption.
- Balances metabolism, helps calcium deficiencies and purifies the lymph system and related organs.
- Helps boost the immune system.
- Helps with insomnia, throat issues, vocal cords, larynx, and digestive disorders.

Chakras: Throat Chakra, Root Chakra.

Kunzite

Stone of Benefits

- Kunzite helps with any soul work you need/want to do.
- Named after a specialist in gemstones who had spent a lot of time cataloging and describing the properties of this special crystal.
- Fosters alignment and healing of chakras in relation to karmatic aspects of life.

Metaphysical Healing Properties:

- Kunzite helps calm your nerves when you are getting ready for an examination or an interview.
- Will help you find out how to look after yourself without the help of anyone else.
- Provides loving energy for the health of your heart, so that you can reflect it back to others.
- Good for your physical health as well as the general health.
- Helps you to keep focusing on your heart chakra and unconditional love.
- Helps alleviate stress and dissolves heart tension that leads to helping solve joint problems.

Physical Healing Properties:

- Relieves heartbreaks and heartache from recent traumas.
- Helps attract healthy romance and loving friendships into your life.
- Helps you work on your compassion, kindness, and tolerance.
- Could reduce menopause effects and solve gynecological problems that you have yet to get checked out.
- Can reduce schizophrenia 's side effects.
- Assists in removing resistance, helps you open up and learn how to commit to bigger things.

Chakra: Heart Chakra.

Tiger eye
Stone of Relativity

- Was made from the psychic miner protector asbestos, wonderful for business.
- First discovered in South Africa.
- In the Greek language, it means "false form."

Metaphysical Healing Properties:

- Helps you find your emotional balance in life.
- Can help harmonize people with different points of view, religious beliefs or approaches to life. It is an excellent contribution to bringing the family together and the relationship's harmony.
- Help you to keep your distance from external influences that can negatively influence or affect you. Mitigates the influence of stressful moods and situations.

Physical Healing Properties:

- Strengthens your blood to support your general vitality.
- Strengthens the endocrine system and helps balance your hormones and biochemistry.
- Can aid in heavy pain relief.
- Slows the energy flow in the body and dampens the excitement of the nerves and the stimulation of the adrenal glands.
- Helps to improve general eyesight and can over time heal eyesight completely.

Chakra: Solar Plexus Chakra, Sacral Chakra, Base Chakra.

Lapis Lazuli

Stone of Relief

- Can help to bring out one's internal truth and is also very protective from negative entities that could live among you.
- helps you recognize the vibration of truth and works to resonate enlightenment within yourself.
- The powerful blue stones are designed to open the third eye and stimulate the pineal gland.
- The Persian word " Lazar" means " blue stone."

Metaphysical Healing Properties:

- Helps to alleviate anger and negative thoughts, as well as to intensify growth of your intuition.
- Creates depth and better clarity in your thinking and communication with yourself and other people
- Will clarify your mind and set your imagination free. Encourage better self-care in your life.
- Helps move your consciousness beyond the worldly and allows you to identify habits, patterns, and lessons that may be difficult to perceive consciously and that may block you from spiritual advancement.

Physical Healing Properties:

- May help to cure problems associated with hearing loss and vertigo.
- Will help your immune, breathing, and nervous system immensely.
- Especially known to help ease migraines.
- Very common in nerve calming and anxiety.

- Helps identify karmic disease roots, otherwise known as karmatic issues in the ancestry of one's family.
- Can help to detect habitual patterns and emotions that sabotage the healing process.
- Aids the endocrine system, migraines, lymph glands, ears, and reduces pain and inflammation in the nasal passages, also are thought to be good for autism and Asperger's syndrome.

Chakra: Third eye Chakra, Throat Chakra.

Vitalite

Stone of Compromise

- Stone affected by various mineral traces such as Quartz, Muscovite and Plemontite.
- Recognized as the stone with the strongest energy release.
- Provides a cleansing influence.

Metaphysical Healing Properties:

- Fosters love and courage, two of the most important virtues of the heart.
- Stimulates a general sense of well-being and helps to reduce anxiety, stress, depression and/or irritability.
- Can dislodge repressed emotions, but it has such a positive influence it rarely takes the form of anger even though it helps absorb repressed negative emotions.
- Currents from this stone may help clear the way to a healthier flow of energy throughout the body.
- Known as the generosity stone.

Physical Healing Properties:

- This stone has such a strong chi, that it affects the whole body at the cell level and promotes a healthy flow of life in every cell, organ, and system.
- Vitalizes the flow of energies to the heart, bringing new vitality not only to the heart but also to the circulatory system, lungs, liver, and digestive system.
- Speaks to the consciousness of the cell, pushes the cells to live, and exist in a joyful, flowing energy.

Chakra: Throat Chakra, Heart Chakra.

Smoky Quartz
Stone of Psychic Protection

- Grounding and anchoring stones, these stones are highly protective and at all times and they are excellent for us all to keep in our aura.

Metaphysical Healing Properties:

- Highly beneficial for you to use and transmute energy when you need protection against any kind of negativity.
- Wonderful for bringing prosperity, abundance, and attraction of good health into your life.
- Can boost your spiritual growth and help clarify your thinking, initially helping you to make any process in your life easier to proceed.

Physical Healing Properties:

- Relaxes pain anywhere in the body.
- Helps soothe cramps and soothe on edge nerves.
- It also helps to relieve headaches, benefits the heart, absorbs electromagnetic, electronic radiation, and facilitates spasms.

Chakra: Root Chakra.

Lazurite

The Stone of Self Awareness

- This composition forms Lapis lazuli mineral when combined with pyrite and calcite.
- Mined in Afghanistan for more than 6,000 years.
- it was used as a pigment in painting and tissue dyeing since at least the sixth or seventh centuries.

Metaphysical Healing Properties:

- Encourages self-consciousness, dynamism, honesty, and straightforwardness.
- Helps you to face the truth and be able to accept it while expressing your own opinion at the same time.
- brings a disturbed mind balance, calmness, and strength to become undisturbed.
- Grants you wisdom and helps to reveal your own inner truth to yourself. Can help balance your physical and spiritual aspects of life so that they can work in harmony together.

Physical Healing Properties:

- Heals neck, larynx, and vocal chord problems.
- Lowers blood pressure and helps to properly regulate thyroid gland function.
- known to prolong the menstrual cycle if needed.
- Restores harmony between the brains hemispheres.
- Helps to cure you of dyslexia and schizophrenia disorders.

Chakra: Heart Chakra, Solar Plexus Chakra.

Calcite

Stone of Achievement

- A hexagonal structure means that calcite is a mineral that helps you to achieve your desires, so it is excellent for manifestation work.
- Brings a huge increase in good vibes to your life.

Metaphysical Healing Properties:

- Clears blockages and helps to remove lingering negative body energy.
- Enhance your memory.
- Amplifies and projects positive energy.
- Bring your life some hope and daily motivation.
- Helps to combat laziness so that you can be more energetic on all levels.

Physical Healing Properties:

- Cleans the removal organs such as the bladder, intestines, and kidneys.
- Helps in calcium absorption throughout the body, especially if you have calcium deficiencies.
- Strengthens the immune system and promotes the growth of under-dimensional children.
- Strengthens the joints and the skeleton.

Chakra: Root Chakra, Throat Chakra.

Labradorite

Stone of Magic

- Known as a stone of magic, and for awakening within your mystical and magical abilities and psychic powers.

- Can be used to bring amazing changes to multiple aspects of your life.

Metaphysical Healing Properties:

- Seals and helps prevent leaks of energy.
- This crystal will help you to recharge mentally, physically, and spiritually.
- Brings synchronicity and serendipity to you.
- Can help to uncover unconscious and subconscious patterns of belief that create unpleasant emotions within you.
- Guides you to understand your own relationship with yourself or with others.

Physical Healing Properties:

- Can help reveal the nature of 'mystery diseases.' The patterns that have created the disease can be revealed over time with this stone.
- Beneficial to the general eye, nerve, brain, bone and spinal cord health.
- Relieves recent stress and controls metabolism.
- This stone helps in rebalancing the sharing of chemicals in your brain, particularly those with cerebral paralysis, sclerosis, optic neuritis, Parkinson's disease, psychotic episodes, and retinal problems.
- Known for treating the common cold, gout, rheumatism, balancing hormones and menstrual tension relief.

Chakra: Throat Chakra, Third eye, Crown Chakra.

Emerald

Letting Go Stone

- These crystals create only positive actions and outcomes; they help to give you the strength to overcome any problems in your everyday life.
- Highly sought after and one of the most valued stones today.

Metaphysical Healing Properties:

- Calms your emotions when upset and generates positive vibrations throughout your body.
- Relieves stress and improves your memory to give you clarity and comprehension.
- Encourages prosperity, wealth, growth, peace, patience, love, harmony, faithfulness, and honesty into your life.
- Ensures an emotional, physical, and mental balance.

Physical Healing Properties:

- Helps you to recover from diseases and infections you may have recently had.
- Heals sinus, congestion, problems with the lungs, clears the eyes and aids in repairing your vision.
- Reinforces your spine and back muscles.
- Detoxifies the heart, liver, and spleen.
- Helps respiratory problems and heart problems. If you have swollen lymph nodes, Emeralds are recommended for you. Even can help spikes in diabetes and hypoglycemia in blood sugar.

Chakra: Solar Plexus, Heart Chakra, Root Chakra.

Crystals for Zodiacs

If you are a follower of astrology and universe signs, you know that each sign has a particular gem, flower, and animal associated with it.

Here are the Gems:

Aquarius: Amethyst, Hematite, Amber.

Pisces: Opal, Amethyst, Bloodstone, Aquamarine, Fire Opal, Coral.

Aries: Aquamarine, Fire Agate, Citrine, Bloodstone, Diamond, Jade, Emerald.

Taurus: Diamond, Carnelian, Chrysocolla, Blue Tourmaline, Rose Quartz.

Gemini: Aquamarine, Rusticated Quartz, Blue Sapphire, Jade, Emerald, Pearl.

Cancer: Ruby, Moonstone, Opal, Fire Opal, Carnelian.

Leo: Amber, Citrine, Jasper, Garnet, Diamond, Carnelian.

Virgo: Watermelon Tourmaline, Smoky Quartz, Moss Agate, Amethyst, Geodes.

Libra: Tourmaline, Rose Quartz, Bloodstone, Jade, Citrine, Opal, Moonstone.

Scorpio: Moldavite, Turquoise, Moonstone, Malachite, Peridot, Opal, Ruby.

Sagittarius: Obsidian, Lapis lazuli, Azurite, Topaz, Smoky Quartz, Turquoise, Chalcedony.

Capricorn: Jade, Tigers Eye, Green Tourmaline, Black Tourmaline, Smoky Quartz, Garnet.

CHAPTER 8
Crystal Mining And Collecting For Yourself

Sometimes you go crystal hunting for hours on end and you can't seem to find anything, a lot of work has been put into this hunt. Other times you barely dig into the earth and you find something that really catches your eye or is of value.

How to go about crystal hunting:
This largely depends on where you live. In some countries, access to mines is strictly forbidden, that is not recommended at all. But in some countries, there are privately owned mines that you can visit by paying a small entrance fee.

If you decide to go crystal hunting, make sure you are dressed appropriately and prepared for the occasion. Crystal mining season usually depends on the weather, but most prospectors prefer spring or autumn when the earth is still moist. Make sure you bring water, a light meal, sturdy shoes, and a charged headlamp no matter the occasion.

Birthstones

Garnet – January

Amethyst – February

Aquamarine – March

Diamond – April

Emerald – May

Pearl – June

Ruby – July

Peridot – August

Sapphire – September

Pink Opal – October

Citrine – November

Turquoise – December

Chakra Balancing Stones

Root Chakra – Alexandrite, fire opal, garnet, red carnelian, red jasper, red tiger's eye, red tourmaline, rhodochrosite, rhodonite, ruby.

Sacral Chakra – Amber, orange calcite, citrine, orange carnelian, sunstone, tiger's eye, topaz.

Solar Plexus Chakra – Amber, citrine, golden calcite, honey, calcite, pyrite, sunstone, tigers eye, topaz, yellow jasper.

Heart Chakra – alexandrite, aventurine, bloodstone, green calcite, emerald, green fluorite, green obsidian, green tourmaline, jade, malachite, moldavite, moss agate, peridot.

Throat Chakra – Angelite, Azurite, Blue Goldstone, Blue Lace Agate, Blue Obsidian, Kyanite, Labradorite, Lapis lazuli, Sapphire.

Third eye Chakra – Apatite, Lapis lazuli, Sugilite, Tranzanite.

Crown Chakra – Amethyst, Ametrine, Charoite, Purple Fluorite, Purple Agate, Sugilite.

Stones to Attract or Enhance

Calm – Rose Quartz
Confidence and Courage – Agate, Bloodstone, Dacite, Carnelian, Charoite, Diamond, Hematite, Tigers Eye
Communication – Blue and green stones: Amazonite, Aquamarine, Blue Lace Agate, Turquoise
Creativity – Yellow for intellect: Calcite, Citrine, Opal, Topaz, Green for growth: Amazonite
Energy – fiery red and orange stones: Carnelian, Garnet Red Jasper

Family harmony – Clusters
General health – Emerald, Aventurine, Green Calcite, Green Tourmaline, Malachite
Happiness – Orange Calcite, Sunstone, Blue Kyanite
Love – Amber, Amethyst, Diamond, Emerald, Jade, Lapis Lazuli, Malachite, Moonstone, Opal, Pearl, Rose Quartz, Sapphire, Topaz, Tourmaline, turquoise
Money – Aventurine, Emerald, Green Tourmaline, Jade, Malachite, Citrine, Golden Calcite. Pyrite, and Tigers Eye
Psychic ability – Amethyst, Clear Quartz
Sex – Ruby and Garnet

Stones to Repel or Eliminate

Addiction – Amethyst
Anger – Amethyst, Carnelian, Emerald, Green Calcite, Green Tourmaline, Topaz
Anxiety – Rose Quartz, Rhodochrosite, Rhodonite, Peridot, Aventurine
Depression – Blue Agate, Kunzite, Amber, Topaz
Fear – Onyx, Smoky Quartz
Heartbreak – Rose Quartz
Jealousy – Peridot, Chrysoprase
Nightmares – Amethyst
Stress – Black Tourmaline, Hematite, Obsidian, Smoky Quartz, Rhodochrosite, Rhodonite

CHAPTER 9
Benefits Of Crystal And Energy Healing

Energy Healing Benefits

One of the greatest benefits of healing energy is stress reduction and relaxation, which triggers the natural healing skills of the body and improves and maintains health. Energy healing is a natural therapy that smoothly balances the life force of the body and gives the recipient health and wellness.

Energy healing is excellent for the healing of all physical, mental, emotional or spiritual problems. Some health benefits include:

- Aids better sleep
- Blood pressure reduction
- Can help with acute injuries and chronic problems (asthma, eczema, headaches, etc.) and medication breakage aids.
- Relieves pain
- Removes energy blockages
- Assists the body in the cleansing of toxins
- Supports the immune system
- Increases vitality
- Increases the frequency of vibration

When we are relaxed and stress-free, we are able to restore our natural ability to heal. To keep the positive energy flowing and the body healing itself, we can turn to crystal healing which is affordable, beneficial, and fascinating to learn about.

Crystal Healing Benefits

Crystals have been used to release physical, mental, and spiritual blockages. Crystals come from the earth, and so when placed on the body, they can help you connect to the healing energies of the planet. The belief is that there is a resonance between crystals and humans. Each crystal has its own healing properties. If a body part or the emotions are affected by stress or illness, the whole body gets affected. The unique healing vibrations need to be introduced to your body to bring it back into balance.

Holistic healing techniques, which include crystal healing, encourage us to rely on our intuition, to listen to the things our soul is trying to tell us, to feel our emotions and nurture our spirit.

How can crystals strengthen our spirit? They can do so by bringing you into alignment with your true self through aura and chakra balancing, through helping you develop your intuition, and through cleaning up and protecting your living space. All of this will help raise your vibrations and contribute to a general sense of well-being.

Crystals and Their Healing

Stones like rose quartz, jade, and amethyst carries a belief in crystal therapy that it can all connect individually with the energy flow of the human body and can help realign the energy channels that interrupt the positive flow of energy that should help the body heal itself.

Red Crystals: Red crystals activate, energize and stimulate. They are related to your ability to use practical skills on a daily basis. They strongly symbolize life, love, and physical vitality. Red stones can help speed up cell growth, release stiffness, and motivate you to improve your love life physically.

Pink Crystals: Pink crystals exude a soft and gentle energy, making them have a calm way of pushing things towards a resolution. Pink brings emotions and sensitivity to our daily actions, it shows the universal color of love and it is excellent for a better and happier life filled with love, affection, and happiness.

Orange Crystals: Orange crystals combine energizing and focusing qualities to give birth to creative and artistic abilities. Used to encourage you to use your personal power, which makes them very beneficial to people who can use a little more self-confidence and self-esteem.

Yellow Crystals: Yellow is the color of the sun, life force, and vitality. Yellow crystals have to do with the function of the body's nervous, digestive and immune systems. Stress, fear, satisfaction, and positivity are all associated with this color. They will bring in more energy and make you feel more uplifting about life.

Green Crystals: Green symbolizes the beauty of life and embraces the abundance and the energies of nature. These crystals are directly associated with the heart. They balance emotions and relationships, promote personal space and growth and create a sense of tranquility. It looked like a restful color.

Light Blue Crystals: Blue is the color of sincerity, inspiration, and spirituality. Light blue crystals and thus all forms of communication are associated with the throat. Taste, sight, smell, feel, hear, feel. Your internal communication is the most important because it is the way you deal with yourself and talk to each other, your thoughts and your ability to express yourself are all influenced by the vibration of light.

Indigo Crystals: Dark blue strengthen your self-esteem and promotes your well-being. Indigo crystals are connected to the third chakra of your eye. Indigo is attributed to perception, understanding, and intuition as well as a profound sense of peace.

Violet Crystals: Violet identifies with mystical and purifying qualities. Violet crystals inspire, fancy, empathy and a sense of service to others. Violet and purple stores help to balance extremes in the body's systems so that they can be useful if you are not sure about the nature of the problem. These crystals are often used for meditation to increase your psychic awareness and strengthen your connection to your higher self.

White Crystals: Clean or white stones are controlled by the moon and represent the potential to reflect all the energy around them. White has to do with the concepts of clarity, protection, and purification. They are linked to sleep and psychological energy and attract fortune and protect.

Black Crystals: While white rocks reflect light and clarity, black rocks absorb light. White reflects the visible, black shows you the hidden potential. Black manifests and solidifies. It holds all energies in itself quietly and therefore requires patience to fully explore. Black stones usually ground, acting as energy anchors to help you get back to normal working conditions. Many things will also reveal hidden aspects so that they can be handled, black stones play a purifying role in this respect and are the most misunderstood of all crystals.

CONCLUSION

Thank for making it through to the end of *Crystals for Beginners*, let's hope it was informative and able to provide you with all of the tools you need to achieve your goals whatever they may be. I hope that you learned a thing or two about the intricacies of crystal healing and how it can benefit you, your life, your relationships, and your reality. Remember to use this book to submit yourself to the positivity of the universe with each healing session. This way, you can harness the powers of the stars and all of the nature around you, bringing you to newer heights in all aspects of your life, and revealing new truths and strengths that can help you meet the height of your spiritual, physical, emotional, and cognitive potential.

The next step is to stop reading and get started doing what you need to do in order to ensure that you are staring/expanding your journey to a more enlightened life through crystal use. You will have better end results the more you practice and the more knowledge you take in on the subject. This book is simply for beginners; how deep you dive into crystals is all up to you!

Studies show that working with crystal can provide you with hundreds of positive benefits for the physical, mental, and emotional bodies when used correctly. You have to put minimal dedication into crystal healing but you do have to put in effort when really trying to access higher consciousness and health benefits associated with doing so. Once you have read this book, reevaluated your life, and thought about ways to begin the process... Give it a try! It could be the best thing you've ever done for yourself.

Finally, if you found this book useful in any way, a review on Amazon is always appreciated!

DESCRIPTION

If you want to start working with crystals and types of beneficial healing but don't know where or how to begin, then *Crystals for beginners* is the book that you have been looking for!

This book discusses every aspect of mind, body, and soul. If you are interested in crystals, it is really important that you know how to choose them, use them and integrate them into your consciousness. Stones can be more powerful sometimes than we can believe. Chakras, energy healing and crystal healing are subjects that many people don't get into, most people don't even know that they exist to such a positive extent.

Crystals and gaining a perspective on your higher consciousness is always a good way to become more in tune with yourself and the earth. There are so many ways you can go about incorporating crystals into your daily / weekly routine. Rebalancing the mind, body, and soul is important to the human condition. Keep your crystals cleansed, keep them safe, and keep them close. Once you're done reading this book go tell your friends about what you've learned, it is always good to help give the people you spend time with a perspective on the matter as well.